Poetry Writing

Theme and Variations

David Starkey
North Central College

NTC Publishing Group
a division of NTC/CONTEMPORARY PUBLISHING GROUP
Lincolnwood, Illinois USA

Sponsoring Editor: Marisa L. L'Heureux
Editor: Lisa A. De Mol
Art Director: Ophelia Chambliss
Production Coordinator: Denise Duffy Fieldman
Cover Art: John S. Dykes, Stock Illustration Source

Acknowledgments begin on page 235, which is to be considered an extension of this
copyright page.

ISBN (student edition): 0-8442-0343-2
ISBN (instructor's edition): 0-8442-0344-0

Published by NTC/Contemporary Publishing Group,
a division of NTC/Contemporary Publishing Group, Inc.,
4255 West Touhy Avenue,
Lincolnwood (Chicago), Illinois 60646-1975 U.S.A.

Library of Congress Cataloging-in-Publication data
Starkey, David, 1962–
     Poetry writing : theme and variations / David Starkey.
          p. cm.
     Includes index.
     ISBN 0-8442-0343-2 (pbk.)
     1. English language—Rhetoric. 2. Poetry—Authorship problems, exercises, etc.
3. Creative writing problems, exercises, etc.
I. Title.
PE 1408.S686   19999
808.1—dc21
                                                                                    99-21611
                                                                                    CIP

9 0 VL 0 9 8 7 6 5 4 3 2 1

Contents

Preface

Chances are that *Poetry Writing: Theme and Variations* has come into your hands because you have enrolled in a creative writing class. If this is the case, you are not alone: many high schools and nearly all American colleges and universities offer at least one course in the subject. Yet creative writing programs are a recent invention, dating back only to the founding of the Iowa Writers' Workshop in the 1930s.

Before that, most poets were pretty much on their own. Chaucer learned his craft by reading Boccaccio; Shakespeare read Marlowe (and just about everybody else); Pope read Dryden; Keats read Wordsworth; and so on. As like as not, the teachers a young poet admired were either deceased or too distant to learn from in person. In lieu of personal instruction, beginning writers quite naturally turned directly to the poetry of those who were more experienced. Often the apprentice's work was a shameless (probably clumsy) imitation. Gradually, however, the more dedicated poets developed their own voices, and they came to look back on their early imitations as crucial steps in their progress as writers. Indeed, one could even argue, as in fact Harold Bloom has, that many poets spend their entire careers "rewriting" the poems of their most important predecessors.

Of course, good poets today still scrutinize the work of their precursors—immediate and far removed. Yet in the last several decades many younger writers have come to see close reading and modeling as less necessary components in a poet's education. "Imitation"—even in the broadest sense of the word, as it is applied in this textbook—is no longer chic.

Granted, not everyone is happy about this development. In fact, it is difficult to find an article by a senior creative writing professor in, say, *The Writer's Chronicle* or *Poets and Writers Magazine* that does not lament the fact that young writers no longer read as much as they once did. Even if we acknowledge that the older generation will always find some reason to grumble about the younger, it is worth thinking carefully about this particular complaint.

I know that my own students often question my insistence on making reading such an integral part of my creative writing courses, and as a new creative writer you may share their reservations. If you are like the majority of my students, you may fear that your voice will be overwhelmed by the stronger voices of the established poets you read. You may feel strongly that you want to write like "yourself," not someone long dead, that tradition is a roadblock to self-discovery rather than a bridge to excellence. If this is the case, you have inherited an attitude that has filtered down from some of the Beat poets of the 1950s and 1960s (who in turn drew on ideas expressed by the Romantic poets of the early nineteenth century). This point of view insists that *personal experience* rather than *literature* should be the determining influence on what a writer writes and how she writes about it.

Up to a point, I am sympathetic to this perspective. The Golden Age of Bad Poetry in our language probably took place in England in the early eighteenth century. Versifiers like William Shenstone, Colley Cibber, Lewis Theobald, and the many other poets who were reviled in Alexander Pope's two versions of *The Dunciad,* composed pieces that consist almost entirely of language and images lifted wholesale from previous poems. These writers seem never to have had an original thought of their own.

Unfortunately, beginning creative writing students in twentieth-century America sometimes have the opposite problem: they rely exclusively on their life experiences without ever becoming acquainted with literature. Ironically, when these students try to write from experience, they end up resorting to the same sorts of clichés as Shenstone and company: the sun smiles sweetly, old age is like winter, love is as sharp as a knife, and so on. As one of my fellow poets once told me, "When you don't know what's already been written, you can never write anything new."

My belief in the importance of writing from models stems from my own experience. Like many writers of my generation, I have a Master of Fine Arts degree in creative writing. I earned mine at Louisiana State University, but my real education as a poet began on the west side of Los Angeles a couple of years before I moved to Baton Rouge. Although I was working as a claims adjuster for an insurance company, I spent much of my spare time in the Santa Monica and Culver City public libraries, both of which have substantial collections of contemporary American poetry. I read and read and read. And—sometimes consciously, sometimes not—I copied the poets I was reading. A childhood anecdote by Elizabeth Bishop or a lyric about a love affair gone wrong by Richard Hugo would inspire poems on similar subjects to come sputtering from my old Smith-Corona electric. I freely admit that my poems were never as good as their models, but that did not matter. I had teachers who could show me where my poetry was strongest and where it failed most grievously. I had someone who could tell me what to write about when I was full of the spirit of poetry but did not know exactly how to give it an outlet—a problem, I later discovered, that is common to beginning poets.

Since those days I have had teachers who have asked me to model my work on other poets, and I frequently ask my students to write responses to poems we have read in class. However, I have never found a classroom text that has this time-honored method of composition as its central focus. *Poetry Writing: Theme and Variations* is designed to fill this need. At its core, the book is an anthology of fifty poems, representing some of the best poetry written by Americans during this century. The poems cover a range of historical periods and styles: from the supple blank verse of Robert Frost's "Birches" to Lyn Hejinian's Language-oriented prose poem, "When one travels, one might 'hit' a storm"; from Frank O'Hara's off-the-cuff observations about Lana Turner in "Poem" to Wendy Rose's denunciation of cultural imperialism in "For the White Poets Who Would Be Indian."

Although I would argue that the best poets tend to be the most widely read, this book is focused only on twentieth-century American poetry. Above all, this is for practical reasons. When you read poetry in class, especially if you are a college English major taking lots of literature classes, the work tends to be anything but contemporary. While almost everyone encounters Shakespeare in high school and college, few people are ever assigned the work of Muriel Rukeyser or Charles Bernstein, and it is crucial, I believe, for the next generation of American poets to know what has been written more recently, to get a feel for the plasticity and zest of our vernacular in the hands of contemporary masters. As any reader of the eighteenth-century poets mentioned above can attest, there is no faster way to torpedo one's poetry than to use flowery, archaic diction. Whatever the faults of the following poems, such diction is hardly ever a concern.

ORGANIZATION

The organization of *Poetry Writing: Theme and Variations* is simple enough. Each chapter begins with a brief overview of the sort of poem you will be asked to write and a discussion of the model poem. Then there is a bridge section linking that poem with a student response. Important literary terms are often introduced in this section. These terms (also included in the glossary at the end) are discussed in conjunction with either the model poem or the student response, but they are rarely the chapter's focus. One of *Poetry Writing*'s central assumptions is that, while it is important for you to learn some of the basic technical aspects of poetry, it is even more important that you write poems. My experience tells me that textbooks that linger over minutiae tend to turn students away from poetry. Therefore, you are generally asked to look at the rhetorical, rather than the formal, emphasis of the model poem.

Most chapters contain only one student response. However, when these poems are especially short, or the assignment is more difficult than usual, I have sometimes included two student pieces to suggest the range of possible approaches to the prompt. If, occasionally, a student poem strikes you as less than ideal, it is worth remembering that the student poems *are* written by students. Their responses represent honest, intelligent attempts to come to terms with the assignments. Some of the contributors to this book were already experienced poets when they began participating in this project, but others had not written poetry since grammar school.

The final section of each chapter is entitled "Your Turn." This section explains the writing prompt in more detail and guides you toward a response of your own. (Every once in a while you may start writing and find yourself veering away from the stated assignment. If that happens, and you feel you are headed in an interesting and productive direction, by all means follow the path you are blazing.)

The chapters are arranged chronologically by the model poet's year of birth. This is to help give you a sense of the development of American poetry in this century. The appendix, "A Brief Introduction to Twentieth-Century American Poetry," also provides information about the poets in the book; it attempts to place them in context and to indicate some of their most important publications and awards. If historical continuity is important to you, you may decide to work conscientiously from E. A. Robinson to Gary Soto. Moreover, basic terminology is generally introduced in the earlier rather than the later chapters. However, you should be able to open up the book to Chapter 50 and write a poem, so there is no reason you cannot skip around if you choose to do so.

Finally, remember that although this book includes the poetry of many of our country's finest poets, you should view them as fellow writers, not godlike beings looking down from Olympus. After all, once you begin working variations on their themes, it will become your turn to carry on the tradition.

ACKNOWLEDGMENTS

Thanks are due to the students in my own and other people's creative writing classes for their diligent work in responding to the model poems in this book. Without them—especially the North Central College students enrolled in English 374 during Spring Term 1998—this book would have been impossible.

Thanks also to these friends and fellow teachers around the country who put me in touch with their talented students: Cindy Gonzales, Ava Leavell Haymon, Jim Peterson, and Mona Lisa Saloy. Likewise, thanks to the reviewers who read the manuscript and offered their guidance, including: Scott Fisher, Rock Valley College; Allison Joseph, Southern Illinois University; James Smith, Armstrong Atlantic State University; and I. C. Storey, Central Michigan University.

I'm especially grateful to Kim Wheatley, my student intern at North Central College. Kim's research and office skills were vital to the preparation of this book. I am also grateful to my editor at NTC, Lisa De Mol, for nudging me in directions that ultimately proved productive and for respecting my vision of the book's overall purpose and scope. Lisa's patience, flexibility, and intelligence are much appreciated.

David Starkey

Chapter One

Talking to Oneself

In this chapter you will create a character and put that person in a situation where she or he can talk aloud to herself or himself. You may describe the character in the third person, or you may even employ some version of yourself as the narrator. The situation should be dramatic, that is, it should force the speaker to confront uncomfortable thoughts and feelings. As you read the two poems in this chapter, think about how you will convey your own character's emotions.

Briefly, the facts of the first poem are these: Climbing a hill above the town where he lives or used to live, an old man pauses to drink, sing, and reminisce aloud to himself about the past. Yet the title of Robinson's poem, "Mr. Flood's Party," is obviously ironic, for there is only one person in attendance, and even he does not seem to be having much fun.

Granted, Robinson tries to endow his pitiful protagonist with a modicum of heroism—Flood is like a knight wearing "A valiant armor of scarred hopes outworn"—but it is clear that the old man is long past his prime: "There was not much that was ahead of him, / And there was nothing in the town below." If our sympathy is with Eben Flood, as Robinson intends, it is because we know that the uncertain future may hold an equally lonely old age for us.

Mr. Flood's Party

Old Eben Flood, climbing alone one night
Over the hill between the town below
And the forsaken upland hermitage
That held as much as he should ever know
On earth again of home, paused warily.
The road was his with not a native near;
And Eben, having leisure, said aloud,
For no man else in Tilbury Town to hear:

"Well, Mr. Flood, we have the harvest moon
Again, and we may not have many more;
The bird is on the wing, the poet says,
And you and I have said it here before.
Drink to the bird." He raised up to the light
The jug that he had gone so far to fill,
And answered huskily: "Well, Mr. Flood,
Since you propose it, I believe I will."

Alone, as if enduring to the end
A valiant armor of scarred hopes outworn,
He stood there in the middle of the road
Like Roland's ghost winding a silent horn.
Below him, in the town among the trees,
Where friends of other days had honored him,
A phantom salutation of the dead
Rang thinly till old Eben's eyes were dim.

Then, as a mother lays her sleeping child
Down tenderly, fearing it may awake,
He set the jug down slowly at his feet
With trembling care, knowing that most things break;
And only when assured that on firm earth
It stood, as the uncertain lives of men
Assuredly did not, he paced away,
And with his hand extended paused again:

"Well, Mr. Flood, we have not met like this
In a long time; and many a change has come
To both of us, I fear, since last it was
We had a drop together. Welcome home!"
Convivially returning with himself,
Again he raised the jug up to the light;
And with an acquiescent quaver said:
"Well Mr. Flood, if you insist, I might.

"Only a very little, Mr. Flood—
For auld lang syne. No more, sir; that will do."
So, for the time, apparently it did,
And Eben evidently thought so too;
For soon amid the silver loneliness
Of night he lifted up his voice and sang,
Secure, with only two moons listening,
Until the whole harmonious landscape rang—

"For auld lang syne." The weary throat gave out,
The last word wavered; and the song being done,
He raised again the jug regretfully
And shook his head, and was again alone.
There was not much that was ahead of him,
And there was nothing in the town below—
Where strangers would have shut the many doors
That many friends had opened long ago.

E. A. Robinson

As you begin writing poetry, you will want to have some important basic vocabulary at hand. First, and most importantly, you should know that the fundamental unit of composition in poetry is the **line** rather than the sentence. A line of poetry, unlike a line of prose, can be "broken" at any point: it does not need to go all the way to the right margin. The poetic equivalent of the paragraph is the **stanza.** A stanza consists of groups of lines of poetry set off from each other by white space.

Obviously, all poetry does not have to rhyme; in fact, *most* of the poetry written in the second half of the twentieth century *does not* rhyme. However, when poets like E. A. Robinson choose to rhyme, they typically make use of a rhyme scheme. You can figure out the **rhyme scheme** (the pattern of rhymes in a poem) by substituting a letter for the last word in the line. Whenever one end-of-line word in the stanza rhymes with another, you repeat that letter. So, in the first stanza of "Mr. Flood's Party," for instance, the rhyme scheme is *abcbdefe*. Rhymes like "below"-"know" and "near"-"hear" are called **perfect rhymes** because the terminal sounds are the same. In **slant rhyme,** or **near rhyme,** the sounds are nearly, but not exactly, alike. An example of this is in the second and fourth lines of the final stanza: "done"- "alone." "Done"- "alone" is also a **sight rhyme,** or **eye rhyme,** because it *looks* as though it should rhyme exactly, even though it does not.

The pleasures of rhyme are many. Rhyming reinforces the rhythm of a line. It brings closure. When rhymed words are linked in sense as well as sound, there seems to be a synergistic effect: the combined force of the two elements is greater than the sum of their individual effects. Rhyming is also a kind of game; it challenges our ingenuity. Rhyme may play a less important role in contemporary literary poetry, but popular music, whether it is sung or spoken (like rap), depends heavily on rhyme. As critic Helen Vendler points out, "We seem to be born liking things that match."

The danger of rhyming your work is that you will begin using clichés. Because we have heard the same sixty or seventy rhymes our whole lives, we have internalized them and we may regurgitate them unwittingly when we start to rhyme. We know that if two people "grow apart" one of them is bound to end up with a "broken heart," that he will "cry" when she says "goodbye," or she will be "blue" because he was "untrue." And so on. There is no doubt that fresh, inventive rhymes can make a good poem even better. But be careful. Rhyme can also accentuate the bad.

Perhaps to avoid this embarrassing possibility, Beth Sheehan chooses not to rhyme at all. Moreover, in Beth's poem "Screaming," the narrator finds herself in a slightly less extraordinary situation than Eben Flood: she is sitting at her desk trying to write while staring at her computer's screen saver. The internal conflict, however, is just as emotional as the one that takes place in "Mr. Flood's Party." The speaker asks herself a series of questions she is unable to answer: "AND WHY CAN'T YOU THINK / about anything clearly? / WHY CAN'T YOU BELIEVE / in anyone you need?" Ultimately, admitting that "I don't know / myself well enough to think / about who I really want to be," she is left with only one way to release her pent-up tension: "I SCREAM."

Screaming

The stars coming toward me
on the black computer screen
get bigger and explode in my face
they're becoming blurry now
and I can almost make out
a butterfly pattern
in the erupting splotches
and I SCREAM

AND WHY CAN'T YOU THINK
about anything clearly?

WHY CAN'T YOU BELIEVE
in anyone you need?
WHY CAN'T YOU SLEEP
to dream about dreaming?
AND WHY CAN'T YOU SPEAK
in words worth hearing?

And I sit in my unyielding
dorm room desk chair
and try to write something
about me, but I don't know
myself well enough to think
about who I really want to be
And I SCREAM

AND WHY CAN'T YOU THINK
of a life worth living?
WHY CAN'T YOU BELIEVE
in a world worth giving?
WHY CAN'T YOU SLEEP
to rest your grieving?
WHY CAN'T YOU SPEAK
do you believe in anything?

And the room is cold
and the building's asleep
and I want to leap
into the dark sky
and live in the stars
and ride on the wings
of the butterflies—
and I SCREAM

Beth Sheehan

Your Turn

Write a poem that shows a person reacting aloud to an uncomfortable situation. As you revise, ask yourself the following questions: Will your reader be able to recognize the emotions this person is confronting? Will he or she get a clear picture of your character from the description you use? Does your setting contribute to character development? (Beth, for instance, places her narrator in a familiar but frustrating setting—her own writing desk; you may decide on a more exotic locale.) What do you want the reader to feel after finishing your poem?

Since your character is talking to himself or herself, it may help to read your monologue aloud. Keep the passages that sound natural and eliminate those that sound forced.

Chapter Two

A Natural
Metaphor

At the end of this chapter you will be asked to show how your engagement with nature has transformed you in some important way. Initially, this may sound a bit daunting. After all, we tend to associate "nature poetry" with canonical (and long-dead) poets like Blake, Wordsworth, Keats—and Robert Frost. However, Jackie Mitchell's poem "dirt" makes it clear that a poet's encounter with nature does not have to end in a profound revelation. Rather, she shows us that simply by looking around, by picking up a handful of soil, we can find valid material for our poetry.

Although we tend to think of nature as an obvious subject for poetry, it turns out that writing a good nature poem is a difficult task. One obvious problem is that much of the natural world just sits there, rooted in the ground where it is growing. Even animals are chiefly of interest to us only if they can somehow serve as mirrors on humanity. Let's face it: the most interesting nature poems are those that feature *people* interacting with their environment.

Robert Frost seems to acknowledge this in "Birches" when he puts both old and young versions of himself into the poem. He uses a recollection of swinging on birch trees as a child to "launch" into a meditation on the adult world. The poet moves from a memory of the pure joy of this activity to the anguish of the adult world, where one is "weary of considerations," where trees evoke the image of a "pathless wood / Where your face burns and tickles . . . / and one eye is weeping / From a twig's having lashed across it open."

Finally, however, birches become a symbol of hope: "One could do worse than be a swinger of birches," the poet writes. Frost's triumph—in this poem and many others—is that he achieves a connection with nature that is both physical *and* spiritual.

Birches

When I see birches bend to left and right
Across the lines of straighter darker trees,
I like to think some boy's been swinging them.
But swinging doesn't bend them down to stay
As ice-storms do. Often you must have seen them
Loaded with ice a sunny winter morning
After a rain. They click upon themselves
As the breeze rises, and turn many-colored
As the stir cracks and crazes their enamel.
Soon the sun's warmth makes them shed crystal shells
Shattering and avalanching on the snow-crust—
Such heaps of broken glass to sweep away
You'd think the inner dome of heaven had fallen.
They are dragged to the withered bracken by the load,
And they seem not to break; though once they are bowed
So low for long, they never right themselves:
You may see their trunks arching in the woods
Years afterward, trailing their leaves on the ground
Like girls on hands and knees that throw their hair
Before them over their heads to dry in the sun.
But I was going to say when Truth broke in
With all her matter-of-fact about the ice-storm
I should prefer to have some boy bend them
As he went out and in to fetch the cows—
Some boy too far from town to learn baseball,
Whose only play was what he found himself,
Summer or winter, and could play alone.
One by one he subdued his father's trees
By riding them down over and over again
Until he took the stiffness out of them,

And not one but hung limp, not one was left
For him to conquer. He learned all there was
To learn about not launching out too soon
And so not carrying the tree away
Clear to the ground. He always kept his poise
To the top branches, climbing carefully
With the same pains you use to fill a cup
Up to the brim, and even above the brim.
Then he flung outward, feet first, with a swish,
Kicking his way down through the air to the ground.
So was I once myself a swinger of birches.
And so I dream of going back to be.
It's when I'm weary of considerations,
And life is too much like a pathless wood
Where your face burns and tickles with the cobwebs
Broken across it, and one eye is weeping
From a twig's having lashed across it open.
I'd like to get away from earth awhile
And then come back to it and begin over.
May no fate willfully misunderstand me
And half grant what I wish and snatch me away
Not to return. Earth's the right place for love:
I don't know where it's likely to go better.
I'd like to go by climbing a birch tree,
And climb black branches up a snow-white trunk
Toward heaven, till the tree could bear no more,
But dipped its top and set me down again.
That would be good both going and coming back.
One could do worse than be a swinger of birches.

Robert Frost

Perhaps all your poetry is written in **free verse,** that is, poetry with no regular meter or line length. However, it is still useful to understand something about **meter,** the arrangement of words in a poem based on the relative stress of their syllables, and **scansion,** the process of counting the number of stressed and unstressed syllables and analyzing their patterns. Granted, students often find scansion confusing, tedious, or both, and there is no doubt that too much scanning can suck the life out of a poem. Nevertheless, it is helpful to know what poets writing in traditional forms are up to, and the information below can serve as a valuable resource when you need to get your hands on some technical terminology.

In fact, until early in this century, nearly all poets writing in English wrote in meter. "Birches," for instance, is in the most common of all English verse forms, unrhymed iambic pentameter, or **blank verse.** In this meter, an unstressed syllable (_) is followed by a stressed syllable (/). Let's scan the first few lines of "Birches":

_ / _ / _ / _ / _ /
When I | see birch | es bend | to left | and right
_ / _ / _ / _ / _ /
Across | the lines | of straight | er dark | er trees,
_ / _ / _ / _ / _ /
I like | to think | some boy's | been swing | ing them.
_ / _ / _ / _ / _ /
But swing| ing does | n't bend | them down | to stay

You will notice that we are concerned with syllables, not words. Each **foot**—i.e., the basic metrical unit—usually consists of one stressed and one or two unstressed syllables. The iamb (_ /) is the most common foot, but there are a few others you ought to be aware of (the adjective is in parentheses):

trochee (trochaic): / _

anapest (anapestic): _ _ /

dactyl (dactylic): / _ _

spondee (spondaic): / /

pyrrhic (pyrrhic): _ _

Line lengths are also given specific names. We know already that a pentameter line has five feet. The others are as follows (though it should be noted that once you begin writing lines with more than six feet in them, it can be difficult to tell the difference between poetry and prose):

monometer: one foot

dimeter: two feet

trimeter: three feet

tetrameter: four feet

hexameter: six feet

heptameter: seven feet

octameter: eight feet

You should also be aware that Frost's lines are exceptionally regular. Normally, there are variations in the lines, so you must look for the dominant foot in order to accurately describe the poem's meter.

But what does all this mean? If you plan to write in traditional English verse forms, it means a lot. You will not go far until you have mastered these basic terms and ideas.

Like Beth Sheehan in the previous chapter, Jackie Mitchell writes in free rather than formal verse. Instead of the arrangement of stressed and unstressed syllables, Jackie's focus is on the theme that occurs in Frost's poem, which is human interaction with the natural world.

Drawing on childhood memories, Jackie chooses a subject that would seem to have little poetic promise: dirt. Yet Jackie, like Frost, inserts herself into the landscape, so that we have an active human presence to focus on. In fact, the speaker takes on a kind of vegetable quality, so enamored is she of dirt. Like the crops and weeds and the apricot seed she planted in the mud of her father's farm, the poet believes that her growth is aided by dirt.

dirt

dirt
just dirt
Mud pies will hurt your
belly
she tells me as I cradle
one spilling ladle of
rich and chilling
dessert

dirt
just dirt
With dad I work
the soil
to the top. Oil black, tapped,
rises through the gaps
in a gray cracked
crust of

dirt
just dirt
Dust off my gingham skirt
with whopping slaps and ask
mom if after mass
I can play again
a sketching stick
artist in

dirt
just dirt
I work, play, create great
masterpieces that sift
to dust with one gust of

open field wind,
then draw, work, play
again in

dirt
just dirt
Toes in soot, I feel the
roots from the weeds
and trees and I put
a dried apricot seed into
the dirty
dirt
just dirt

Wait and see . . .
It will grow just like me
among these weeds
from the
dirt
just dirt

Jackie Mitchell

Your Turn

First of all, you will need to think of some feature of the natural world: it may be a type of plant, as in Robert Frost's "Birches," a mountain, a river, a lake, or even, as in Jackie's poem, dirt. Then begin writing a poem that shows how your interaction with nature has altered you in a significant way.

Take a cue from the two poets in this chapter and consider placing yourself directly in the poem. Don't try to be too profound. Rather than stating, "Nature has changed me forever!" *show* your involvement. A well-told poem about a satisfying hike in a local forest preserve will be much more convincing to readers than generalizations about "glorious sunsets" or "the mighty ocean."

Chapter Three

Characterizing Place

The poems in this chapter describe places that the poets know very well, places that have special significance for the authors. Indeed, the reason the following poem by Carl Sandburg has managed to hang around for so long when most of his other work is forgotten is that he has managed to make Chicago seem both despicable *and* alluring. Sandburg obviously admires a city that "Under the terrible burden of destiny [laughs] as a young man laughs, / Laughing even as an ignorant fighter laughs who has never lost a battle." Yet he is not afraid to point out the many things that are wrong with Chicago: "They tell me you are wicked and I believe them, for I have seen your painted women under the gas lamps luring the farm boys. / And they tell me you are crooked and I answer: Yes, it is true, I have seen the gunman kill and go free to kill again." The combination of good and bad, light and darkness makes the poem seem whole.

13

Chicago

Hog Butcher for the World,
Tool Maker, Stacker of Wheat,
Player with Railroads and the Nation's Freight Handler;
Stormy, husky, brawling,
City of the Big Shoulders:

They tell me you are wicked and I believe them, for I have
    seen your painted women under the gas lamps luring
    the farm boys.
And they tell me you are crooked and I answer: Yes, it is true
    I have seen the gunman kill and go free to kill again.
And they tell me you are brutal and my reply is: On the
    faces of women and children I have seen the marks of
    wanton hunger.
And having answered so I turn once more to those who
    sneer at this my city, and I give them back the sneer and
    say to them:
Come and show me another city with lifted head singing so
    proud to be alive and coarse and strong and cunning.
Flinging magnetic curses amid the toil of piling job on job,
    here is a tall bold slugger set vivid against the little soft
    cities;
Fierce as a dog with tongue lapping for action, cunning as a
    savage pitted against the wilderness,
    Bareheaded,
    Shoveling,
    Wrecking,
    Planning,
    Building, breaking, rebuilding,
Under the smoke, dust all over his mouth, laughing with
    white teeth,
Under the terrible burden of destiny laughing as a young
    man laughs,
Laughing even as an ignorant fighter laughs who has never
    lost a battle,
Bragging and laughing that under his wrist is the pulse, and
    under his ribs the heart of the people,
    Laughing!
Laughing the stormy, husky, brawling laughter of Youth,
    half-naked, sweating, proud to be Hog Butcher, Tool
    Maker, Stacker of Wheat, Player with Railroads and
    Freight Handler to the Nation.

Carl Sandburg

Writers, critics, and students of literature frequently use the word **imagery** to talk about what is "concrete"—as opposed to "abstract"—in a poem. Of course, all language is necessarily abstract, but if you think of an image as "a picture made out of words" (to use the phrase of British poet C. Day Lewis) you can easily see the distinction. In its broader usage, imagery refers to the other four senses as well: taste, touch, sound, and smell.

Since the earliest recorded poetry, we find writers taking advantage of the image's ability to convey a feeling or idea more forcefully than an abstraction. Indeed, it is often the case that an image is used to make an abstraction concrete. For example, in the phrase "Flinging magnetic curses" in Sandburg's "Chicago," spoken curses (which cannot be seen) become tangible things to be hurled.

It would be difficult to overstate the importance of imagery to poetry. American creative writing programs have held the adage "Show, Don't Tell" as a central, nearly inviolable truth. In fact, many contemporary poets would argue that a poem without vivid and insightful imagery is not a poem at all. Whether or not you are willing to go that far, your own experience with previous poems should convince you that sometimes—to reclaim a cliché—a "picture" is worth a thousand words.

Like Sandburg, Katy Montgomery uses imagery extensively and acknowledges both positives and negatives in "Snowy Sacandaga." The poem, which depicts a vacation spot visited by the poet and her family, focuses on the main recreational activity at Sacandaga, where "metal-rudders swoosh down the hill / and skate far across the lake, just missing / the remains of last summer's bonfire / and the big oak tree to the left." This is clearly a fun place to be, although it is not without its discomforts and hazards. The weather is painfully cold, the winds are "shrieking," and the ride itself is potentially very dangerous.

Incidentally, Katy's poem proves that a writer need not reside in a place for years to be able to write about it well. Although she visited Sacandaga only a single time, Katy's memory of it is as vivid as though she had lived there a long time.

Snowny
Sacandaga

Perched on a hill, a tiny white dwelling
with cinnabar roofing overlooks
the Great Sacandaga Lake—a snowy playground.
Hushed and primeval, the drift-covered lake
melts into the crisp Adirondacks.

Black smoke still floats out of the home
on the hill, and after Christmas, laughter echoes
out of the chimney and through the crisp pines.

Light illuminates the clear, immaculate
icicles that hang from the house's eaves,
and birdseed whisked to the ground by shrieking
winds leaves tiny imprints in the snow.

Sometimes it drifts down so heavy and hard
that piles of magic cushion those
who take the death-drop straight backwards.

On those days, sleds plop rather than fly—
inspiring the innovative to pack in
the snow with bright mittens and ice down
a slippery runway with kitchen water.

Then, metal-rudders swoosh down the hill
and skate far across the lake, just missing
the remains of last summer's bonfire
and the big oak tree to the left.

As night falls, scattered lights gleam
around the glacial phenomenon like candles,
while the die-hards stay out late constructing ramps
to send them soaring into tomorrow.

Katy Montgomery

Your Turn

Now is your chance to write a poem describing a place you know well. Perhaps, like Carl Sandburg, you have recently moved to a new city that ignites your imagination. Or, like Katy Montgomery, you may depict a rural area you love. The important thing is to help your reader share in all its sights, sounds, smells, physical sensations, and tastes. When a writer evokes one or more of the five senses, she connects us immediately to the "real" world. Sandburg and Katy rely heavily on specific details to bring to life the places they know and to distinguish them from everywhere else.

Remember, too, that if you really cherish the location central to your poem, you will try to balance your account with a description of a few things that are *not* perfect (and vice versa, if you dislike the place).

Chapter Four

The Power of Art

The focus of this chapter is art's power to transform the way we see things. For centuries, artists have argued that they can take us out of our ordinary lives, that the artist creates a kind of parallel universe that is both more terrifying and more beautiful than the one we actually inhabit.

One of the themes the poet Wallace Stevens returned to again and again was the notion that art could rearrange and heighten the poignancy of the world around it. In "Anecdote of the Jar," a human creation placed in the middle of rural Tennessee makes the wilderness "no longer wild." Indeed, the jar takes "dominion everywhere." This is a strange thought, that a simple, plain jar—it is, after all, "gray and bare"—can overwhelm the natural world. Yet, intuitively, we recognize Stevens's point: human beings are fascinated by things that other human beings have made.

Anecdote
of the Jar

I placed a jar in Tennessee,
And round it was, upon a hill.
It made the slovenly wilderness
Surround that hill.

The wilderness rose up to it,
And sprawled around, no longer wild.
The jar was round upon the ground
And tall and of a port in air.

It took dominion everywhere.
The jar was gray and bare.
It did not give of bird or bush,
Like nothing else in Tennessee.

Wallace Stevens

Andy Johnson, a singer in a rock-and-roll band, examines the effect of a very different work of art: his voice. In a poem that takes on some of the swagger we expect from rock singers, Andy trumpets the wide variety of sensations his voice can evoke. From touch ("soft, like new jello," "the sting of your mother's hand") to smell ("a fragrance like sweet soap") to taste ("your first kiss under an observant moon") to unexpected sounds ("the vibrations of that tornado siren when you were 12"), Andy's voice, like the jar in Stevens's poem, has authority over everything else around it.

In some ways, these two poems are very different. "The Anecdote of the Jar" is set in the country. It involves a strange, unexplained act, the placing of a jar in the wilderness. Other than the narrator, there are no human agents in the poem to witness what is going on. In contrast, "You Can Ride on the Notes of My Voice" involves what for many of us is a daily event: listening to a rock song. The images are domestic. The settings are familiar.

Yet both poets have in common the belief that anyone who is willing to give himself or herself up to art will be the better for that surrender. That person will understand life in a more profound way than someone who ignores art, because art forces us to re-envision our lives and allows us to find comfort when we need it most.

You can
ride on the
notes of
my voice

You can ride on the notes of my voice.
Go ahead, I don't mind.
They're soft, like new jello.
And a fragrance like sweet soap will fill your head.

With the bass sounds you may recall your first piano recital
Or feel the vibrations of that tornado siren when you were 12.

When my voice grows rough and loud,
You may feel the sting of your mother's hand
On your face, ten years old.

When I sink below a whisper
You may taste your first kiss under an observant moon
In a campground blanketed with smooth night.

When I turn to tenor, feel the swelling pride
Sweaty hands grasping your diploma, 18 years old.
Let your face heat up in that righteous fever.
Go ahead. Let my voice take you where you need to go.

Andrew Johnson

Your Turn

Search your memory or activate your imagination to create a scene in which a particular art—whether it be ceramics or music (as in the two examples above), dance, painting, sculpture, or literature—changes the way the speaker or those around him view the world.

You might, for instance, write a poem about witnessing a break-dancing exhibition in a city park. As the crowd's attention becomes more and more riveted on the dancers, the world around you seems to spin away until the earth's entire gravitational pull appears to emanate from the scene before you.

Or perhaps you recall standing in an art museum in front of a particular painting. All your life you had seen only reproductions in books. Now, suddenly, all your preconceptions are swept away. The canvas is much smaller or larger, the colors much brighter. Everything you have always assumed about the painting—and, indeed, about art itself—has to change.

Chapter Five

3 x 5 Poems

This chapter's focus is the very short poem. Poetry instructors frequently tell their students to condense, to prune, to get rid of every unnecessary word. Although writing less rather than more is harder than it sounds, the following assignment asks you to take that advice seriously.

"This is Just to Say" is one of William Carlos Williams's most widely anthologized poems, and for good reason. In just 29 words he manages to evoke not only a scene—someone leaving a note of apology for eating all the fruit in the "icebox"—but also a relationship. The tone of familiarity suggests love and intimacy between two people who will not be excessively upset by such a minor misdemeanor. We might even be able to make some tentative characterizations about the speaker himself: he sounds mischievous, pleasure-loving, and maybe a little self-satisfied.

This is Just
to Say

I have eaten
the plums
that were in
the icebox

and which
you were probably
saving
for breakfast

Forgive me
they were delicious
so sweet
and so cold

William Carlos Williams

Of course, Williams was writing long before the invention of Post-It™ notes (the poem first appeared in book form in 1934), but "This is Just to Say" is nevertheless an excellent example of the sort of poem that would naturally make use of this new "medium." The two student responses certainly make clever use of the tiny working space. In Heather's poem, we don't know what "that crazy thing" is that the speaker asked of the person she's addressing. However, in such a short poem the lack of specificity works in favor of, rather than against, the poet. Whatever it was, it sounds important. "Forget It" implies many possible situations, none of them comfortable. "Urgent," on the other hand, is humorous. As Kristi points out, the difference between Williams's poem and her own is that "my narrator is simply being absent-minded."

Note that when she is discussing her poem, Kristi refers to "my narrator"; she makes a clear distinction between the person in her poem and herself. Throughout this book we will insist on a similar separation between the author and the speaker. The former is the actual person who sits down and writes the poem. The **speaker,** on the other hand, is the poem's narrator. This may sound like hairsplitting, but frequently an author will employ a speaker who she feels is markedly different from herself. And even when an author claims to be talking about herself, the necessities of writing poetry ensure that the author and the speaker will not be the same person. Poets are always using compression and elision. They condense life's experiences and leave out things that are not essential.

Therefore, the claims made above about the speaker of "This is Just to Say"—that he is "mischievous, pleasure-loving, and maybe a little self-satisfied"—cannot necessarily be applied to Williams himself. Similarly, Heather and Kristi may well have created personas that are nothing like their real selves.

Forget It

I don't need it anymore,
that crazy thing I asked of you,
forget I ever asked.

Heather Cramer

Urgent

Someone called for you
with an urgent plea
to return their call
immediately.

I am sorry but I
did not get
their name
or phone number.

Kristi Yurs

Your Turn

Try writing your own very short poem—one that would fit on a 3″ × 5″ index card. Address the poem to someone you know well. Make sure *every* word is necessary. Can you delete an article or a preposition or an adverb? Can one word serve the function of two or more? Is that appositive really necessary? (An appositive is a noun or noun phrase that renames the noun or pronoun that has preceded it.)

As you can see from the model poems, your tone may range from bitter to comic. Rather than viewing the lack of space as a restriction, try to envision it as an opportunity to hint at things that you would rather not express directly.

Chapter Six

Truce

This chapter focuses on personal arguments and the ways we find to settle them. As you read through the chapter, think of people with whom you have had conflicts and how those conflicts were eventually resolved.

Before discussing the quarrel Ezra Pound (1885–1972) had with Walt Whitman (1819–1892), it is useful to know a little bit about the younger poet. Ezra Pound, one of the great Modernist American poets, played a significant role in shaping the poetry of our century. He helped launch the careers of Robert Frost and T. S. Eliot, among many others. He championed the **imagist movement,** which valued precise imagery in poetry, freedom in the choice of subject matter, and an avoidance of excessive sentimentality. In general, Pound helped shake American poetry free from its slavish imitation of European models, and—though he valued wide learning and cross-cultural sharing of ideas—he is often credited with helping make American poetry distinct from that of all other cultures.

It is ironic, therefore, that he "detests" Walt Whitman, another groundbreaking American poet. Critics have pointed out that part of Pound's resentment came from the fact that he and Whitman were very much alike: they both wanted to be the Great American Poet. Moreover, while we may think of Whitman as a figure from the distant past, he was still very much alive when Ezra Pound was born.

Evolutionary psychologists will tell us that conflict—our willingness to use aggression to get what we want—is an inherent part of human nature. They also say that our ability to compromise is an integral factor in our genetic makeup. If this is true, there seems to be something of the instinctive struggle for territory in Pound's long antipathy toward Whitman, with "Pact" representing Pound's realization that the struggle can never be won. The "father" and "son" are equally strong. It is best, Pound ultimately decides, simply to call a truce, and move on to other battles.

A Pact

I make a pact with you, Walt Whitman—
I have detested you long enough.
I come to you as a grown child
Who has had a pig-headed father;
I am old enough now to make friends.
It was you that broke the new wood,
Now is a time for carving.
We have one sap and one root—
Let there be commerce between us.

Ezra Pound

When one line of poetry runs into the next line without any punctuation to stop it, that line is said to be enjambed. **Enjambment** comes from the Old French word for "straddling" and is sometimes described as an "in-striding." *Enjambment* is a handy term to know because if you write poetry you will inevitably be doing it—even if you don't realize it. In the Pound poem above, the first and second lines are *not* enjambed: "I make a pact with you, Walt Whitman— / I have detested you long enough." We must pause at these **end-stopped** lines, first at the dash, then at the period. However, the third line *is* enjambed. "I come to you as a grown child" strides over to "Who has had a pig-headed father" without any punctuation. Varying your lines between those with end-stopped **line breaks** and those that use enjambment can make for some interesting rhythms and inventive twists of meaning.

Like Pound, Kelly Janssen makes good use of enjambment. Her poem differs from the model poem, though, in that the conflict in "Compromise" is not nearly as abstract as that in "A Pact." Pound's battle is over intellectual turf. He wants to usher in a new era of poetry different from the sort that Whitman wrote. Yet Whitman, of course, cannot respond to Pound's accusation that he is "pig-headed," since Whitman had passed away years before "A Pact" was written. The disagreement essentially takes place inside Pound's head.

Kelly, on the other hand, is at odds with an opponent who is in her face. Her irascible and unreliable brother borrows her CDs and returns them much the worse for wear. Kelly's truce takes the form of a treaty. She will swap music with her brother, provided that he does not leave her disc in his friend's car and that the disc comes back absolutely clean. Should he violate any terms of the treaty, she has explosive ammunition at her fingertips.

Compromise

All right,
you can borrow my Cure CD
if I can listen to your
Depeche Mode, but not
the one with the purple cover,
the one with the song
"Personal Jesus" on it,
and if you forget my disc
in Todd's car again,
you're dead.
If you even so much as
leave a fingerprint on it,
Depeche Mode will no longer
have a home in your collection.
And remember, I saw you
take that ten off Dad's dresser,
so don't forget to return it
by tomorrow before you leave
for school. Any questions?

Kelly Janssen

Your Turn

Think of someone with whom you have had a long quarrel. The quarrel may be relatively distant and intellectual, like Ezra Pound's squabble with Walt Whitman. Or it may, like Kelly's "Compromise," be more immediate and personal, involving an ongoing dispute with a parent, sibling, or friend. In your poem, attempt to come to terms with that person. You don't necessarily have to give in all the way—Pound and Kelly certainly don't—but try, at least, to effect some sort of reconciliation.

If a situation does not come to mind right away, ask yourself the following questions: Who in the world most aggravates me? Short of killing that person, how could I best reach a cease-fire with her or him? What circumstances would have to be in place for that truce to occur? What would the truce entail?

A Place of Hope

As was the case in Chapter Three, Chapter Seven asks you to describe a place that is important to you. This time, however, you will focus on a location that inspires feelings of hope. As always, careful use of details, of sights and sounds and smells, will help your reader share in your sense of refuge and peace and optimism.

Marianne Moore has found her place of hope in a small New England seaside town, although her emotions may not be immediately apparent if this is your first encounter with "The Steeple-Jack." Indeed, reading *any* poem by Moore for the first time can be a little disconcerting. She appears obsessed with describing everything she sees down to its last particular. She uses strange metaphors and erudite references. In the third stanza of "The Steeple-Jack," for instance, she writes of "a sea the purple of the peacock's neck [which has now] / paled to greenish azure [in the same way that] Dürer changed / the pine green of the Tyrol to

27

peacock blue and guinea / gray." Evidently, Moore is alluding to a specific painting (or group of paintings) by the German painter Albrecht Dürer (1471–1528). But if the reader does not know the painting, or does not even know who Dürer is, how enjoyable can the poem be?

The answer to that question need not be *Not very much* if you are willing to give her work a chance. The best way to approach Moore's poetry is simply to pay very close attention to her sentences: more often than not you can figure out what she's talking about. If she loses you, read through the parts that seem over your head and have fun with the rest. A true eccentric, Moore herself was very playful. In her later years, she took to wearing a tricornered hat. She was a huge fan of the Brooklyn Dodgers. Once called the world's greatest living observer, she wrote poems about everything from snails to steamrollers.

The Steeple-Jack
Revised, 1961

Dürer would have seen a reason for living
    in a town like this, with eight stranded whales
to look at; with the sweet sea air coming into your house
on a fine day, from water etched
    with waves as formal as the scales
on a fish.

One by one in two's and three's, the seagulls keep
    flying back and forth over the town clock,
or sailing around the lighthouse without moving their wings—
rising steadily with a slight
    quiver of the body—or flock
mewing where

a sea the purple of the peacock's neck is
    paled to greenish azure as Dürer changed
the pine green of the Tyrol to peacock blue and guinea
gray. You can see a twenty-five
    pound lobster; and fish nets arranged
to dry. The

whirlwind fife-and-drum of the storm bends the salt
    marsh grass, disturbs stars in the sky and the
star on the steeple; it is a privilege to see so
much confusion. Disguised by what
    might seem the opposite, the sea-
side flowers and

trees are favored by the fog so that you have
    the tropics at first hand: the trumpet vine,
foxglove, giant snapdragon, a salpiglossis that has

spots and stripes; morning-glories, gourds,
    or moon-vines trained on fishing twine
at the back door:

cattails, flags, blueberries and spiderwort,
    striped grass, lichens, sunflowers, asters, daisies—
yellow and crab-claw ragged sailors with green bracts—toad-plant,
petunias, ferns; pink lilies, blue
    ones, tigers; poppies, black sweet-peas.
The climate

is not right for the banyan, frangipani, or
    jack-fruit trees; or for exotic serpent
life. Ring lizard and snakeskin for the foot, if you see fit;
but here they've cats, not cobras, to
    keep down the rats. The diffident
little newt

with white pin-dots on black horizontal spaced-
    out bands lives here; yet there is nothing that
ambition can buy or take away. The college student
named Ambrose sits on the hillside
    with his not-native books and hat
and sees boats

at sea progress white and rigid as if in
    a groove. Liking an elegance of which
the source is not bravado, he knows by heart the antique
sugar-bowl shaped summerhouse of
    interlacing slats, and the pitch
of the church

spire, not true, from which a man in scarlet lets
    down a rope as a spider spins a thread;
he might be part of a novel, but on the sidewalk a
sign says C. J. Poole, Steeple Jack,
    in black and white; and one in red
and white says

Danger. The church portico has four fluted
    columns, each a single piece of stone, made
modester by whitewash. This would be a fit haven for
waifs, children, animals, prisoners,
    and presidents who have repaid
sin-driven

senators by not thinking about them. The
    place has a schoolhouse, a post-office in a
store, fish-houses, hen-houses, a three-masted
    schooner on
the stocks. The hero, the student,
    the steeple-jack, each in his own way,
is at home.

It could not be dangerous to be living
    in a town like this, of simple people,
who have a steeple-jack placing danger signs by the church
while he is gilding the solid-
    pointed star, which on a steeple
stands for hope.

Marianne Moore

The majority of the poems in this book are written in free verse. Others, like E. A. Robinson's "Mr. Flood's Party" and Robert Frost's "Birches," are written in traditional English meter. Although she is not alone—later twentieth-century poets like Laurence Lieberman and Molly Peacock have followed her lead—Moore is unusual in that she generally writes her poems using **syllabics.** As the name suggests, such a poem is one in which the poet counts the total number of syllables per line rather than the number of accented syllables. In "The Steeple-Jack," the lines in most of the stanzas have the following syllable count: 11–10–14–8–8–3. As she often did, Moore ornaments her stanzas by indenting the lines in interesting and consistent ways.

Admittedly, she cheats a couple of times—notice, for instance, how in the last line of stanza four ("side flowers and") she makes things simpler by turning "flowers" into a one-syllable word—but on the whole she remains faithful to the pattern she imposes on herself. While this occasionally makes for some less than scintillating line breaks (too often Moore ends on a preposition or an article), this configuration of syllables forces us to read her sentences in fresh and unexpected ways.

Another technique Moore uses extensively in "The Steeple-Jack," especially in the early stanzas describing the town's flora and fauna, is cataloging. The term **catalog,** when used in regard to poetry, means "to make a list." Actually, this is one of the oldest poetic tricks. Homer catalogued warriors in *The Iliad*, as did Virgil in *The Aeneid*. Milton catalogued angels in *Paradise Lost*. More recently, New York poet Ted Berrigan made frequent, and often hilarious, use of the device.

Becky Michelsen carefully studied the complex structure of "The Steeple-Jack," but ultimately decided against using syllabics and cataloging. She wanted her own piece to follow a much simpler form. If Moore's goal is to paint an elaborate canvas in which each person, animal, and plant is distinct, Becky is more like a water colorist. She uses broad strokes and loose washes to suggest a prevailing tone.

Nevertheless, in her poem Becky is just as attentive to the ways that a specific location can affect our mood. Rather than making a long list of the attributes of her favorite spot, Becky devotes her energy to capturing a specific ambience. "My Place" celebrates a quiet moment alone. The speaker, wrapped up in a blanket and concentrating on the sound of rain and her own breathing, is content with just "a handful of thoughts." Becky's source of hope is solitude and direct contact with the natural world.

My Place

Sitting with my back
    to the window
A light rain gently taps
and I know it's time
    to be just with me
Grabbing my blanket
    and a handful of thoughts
I ease out the backdoor
    and into a nook
between the deck and overhang
Wrapping the blanket around me
I take a deep breath and
    inhale the rain
    my nostrils tingling
with the dampness of the air
My mind empties and I watch the rain
    carom off the deck
    the grass bending
struggling
    against the drops
I breathe deeply again
The rain quickens

Becky Michelsen

Your Turn

In her seaside town with its "elegance of which / the source is not bravado," Marianne Moore seems to have found peace. Likewise, in her "nook / between the deck and overhang," Becky has found a space where she feels sheltered.

Write a poem about a place that comforts you and gives you hope. Avoid effusive clichés like "The beach is so special to me!" or "My mind's at ease when I'm under my pine tree." Instead, let Marianne Moore's precise yet fanciful catalogs or Becky Michelsen's quiet description serve as models for your own writing.

Allow yourself plenty of latitude when selecting your place of hope. It may be as large as a town or country, or as small as an alcove in your backyard. And it may not always be available to you. Perhaps you recall somewhere from your childhood that is now gone. Or, as in Becky's case, there may have to be certain weather conditions before you consider the location special.

Chapter Eight

The Birth of Gods

In this chapter you will write a poem in which you imagine the birth of an important religious figure. The model poem is T. S. Eliot's "Journey of the Magi." By the time the poem was published in 1927, T. S. Eliot was well on his way to becoming a devout Anglican. Yet the story he tells of the birth of Christ is not the one found in the Bible. In Matthew 2:10, for instance, when the wise men saw the star, "they rejoiced with exceeding great joy." In the next verse, they are worshiping Jesus; there is nothing specific about their journey.

Here, however, the magus (i.e., one of the three wise men) who is speaking sounds like a real person. He grumbles about the weather (it is too cold) and the help ("the camel men cursing and grumbling / And running away, and wanting their liquor and women"). He's even less than enthusiastic about witnessing one of the most significant events in history: "it was (you may say) satisfactory." And for the speaker the culmination of this long, difficult trip is not joy or contentment, but rather doubt and fear and a kind of despair. When he says in the final line, "I should be glad of another death," we assume he's talking about his own.

Paradoxically, however, the fact that the magus is a three-dimensional character makes the event he was part of all the more moving. Because he has suffered physical and emotional discomfort, we know he is a human being much like ourselves. Clearly, neither he nor the poet feeding him his lines would be willing to settle for a truth that was not hard-earned.

The Journey of the Magi

'A cold coming we had of it,
Just the worst time of the year
For a journey, and such a long journey:
The ways deep and the weather sharp,
The very dead of winter.'
And the camels galled, sore-footed, refractory,
Lying down in the melting snow.
There were times we regretted
The summer palaces on slopes, the terraces,
And the silken girls bringing sherbet.
Then the camel men cursing and grumbling
And running away, and wanting their liquor and women,
And the night-fires going out, and the lack of shelters,
And the cities hostile and the towns unfriendly
And the villages dirty and charging high prices:
A hard time we had of it.
At the end we preferred to travel all night,
Sleeping in snatches,
With the voices singing in our ears, saying
That this was all folly.

Then at dawn we came down to a temperate valley,
Wet, below the snow line, smelling of vegetation;
With a running stream and a water-mill beating the darkness,
And three trees on the low sky,
And an old white horse galloped away in the meadow.
Then we came to a tavern with vine-leaves over the lintel,
Six hands at an open door dicing for pieces of silver,
And feet kicking the empty wine-skins.
But there was no information, and so we continued
And arrived at evening, not a moment too soon
Finding the place; it was (you may say) satisfactory.

All this was a long time ago, I remember,
And I would do it again, but set down
This set down
This: were we led all that way for
Birth or Death? There was a Birth, certainly,
We had evidence and no doubt. I had seen birth and death,
But had thought they were different; this Birth was
Hard and bitter agony for us, like Death, our death.
We returned to our places, these Kingdoms,
But no longer at ease here, in the old dispensation,
With an alien people clutching their gods.
I should be glad of another death.

T. S. Eliot

The word *taboo* comes from the Tongan word *tabu* and refers to the prohibition against violating something sacred. For instance, until the caste system was outlawed in India (and, some would say, even afterwards), it was taboo for members of the highest caste, Brahmins, to have physical contact with members of the lowest caste, the so-called untouchables.

While the notion of a caste system makes many of us uncomfortable, often there are very good reasons for taboos. The taboo against incest, to take just one example, is supported by plenty of sound genetic and social arguments. Sometimes, however, poets feel compelled to break taboos. The nature of this book (it is primarily a student text-book) means that most taboos are respected. Nevertheless, there are times when chapter assignments may enter a gray area. Because you may feel a certain *taboo* associated with writing on this subject, two very different student responses to Eliot's poem are included to give you a better idea of the range of possible reactions to the assignment.

Shannon Daly's "The Savior" is even more enigmatic than Eliot's poem. In a waste-land urban setting, "thick with smells / of oil, tar and sweat," we see a mother holding a crying baby. How she got there and why, we never learn. Likewise, the path the baby will follow to become a "doer of good, / bearer of wisdom, of peace" is a mystery to the reader. So intent on preserving the secret of her protagonist is Shannon that she does not even use the standard capitalization of the pronoun "He," preferring to remain ambiguous about whether or not the child is, indeed, *the* Savior.

Heather Cramer's "Magi at the Marriott," on the other hand, does refer specifically to the second coming of Christ. However, she speculates that present-day magi would not be satisfied with the original accommodations. Instead, she imagines "white linen" hiding "the sticky straw and messy mishaps." Then, after painting a detailed portrait, complete with "tables manned by little waitstaff persons," she undercuts the entire scene with a devastatingly sardonic final stanza.

The Savior

The city was tired.
Sun-roasted, beaten to hell.
Streetlights broken,
restless wind.

The air was thick with smells
of oil, tar and sweat,
crumbling sidewalks,
pot-holed streets.

Abandoned buildings
splattered with paint.
Abandoned cars
in weedy lots.

One mother is all alone.
Her baby cries.
It is he, doer of good,
bearer of wisdom, of peace.

The city was broken,
worn and abused.
It is here that he enters.
It is here that he saves.

Shannon Daly

The Night of the Magi, by Marriott

I imagine all the usual props—
the straw, the manger, the animal stench.
But what if the event was catered by Marriott?

White linen would hide the sticky straw and messy
    mishaps,
Though scented candles all around wouldn't lift the
    barnyard smell.
Food fed to shepherds, wisemen and angels would've been
Fruit, finger sandwiches, juicy meat, and cappuccino on
    that cold night.
Sitting at tables manned by little waitstaff persons,
running to fill the glasses with wine, milk, and tea.
The maroon dress of the Marriott messengers clashing
with the red silk of the ancient wise men.

Of course, this is absurd.
It could never happen.
Who would pay the bill?

Heather Cramer

Your Turn

Write a poem in which you imagine the birth of an important religious figure. It may be the founder of a world religion like Christianity, Islam, Buddhism, Hinduism, or Judaism, or it may be a lesser known or *wholly imaginary* faith. Like the poets in this chapter, you should use concrete sensory details to help your reader fully envision the event. Don't worry about sticking too closely to authoritative texts: the idea of the exercise is to use your own inventiveness to create a vivid scene.

A certain amount of ambiguity will make your poem more complex and more interesting to read. It is unrealistic to simply say, "X was born: all problems are solved." Nearly all world religions acknowledge that bringing even a flawless prophet into a less-than-perfect world will result in some serious challenges. You may, therefore, want to hint at the challenges that will inevitably be faced by both the prophet and his or her followers.

Chapter Nine

In Defiance

The poem you write for this chapter will require that you take a defiant stand toward a person or group of people you feel it is important to oppose. Try to channel your feelings of aggression and enmity into a small vessel—your poem—that can contain them without bursting apart.

An excellent example of intense anger taking a compact, constructive poetic form is Claude McKay's "If We Must Die." This famous sonnet was written during the race riots of 1919 to encourage African Americans to stand up for their rights. During the Second World War, Winston Churchill read the poem to the House of Commons to rally support for the fight against the Germans. In both cases, "If We Must Die" served to inspire a group of people who were unwilling to yield to a powerful foe.

Perhaps the poem's most noticeable rhetorical strategy is the contrast between animals and men. In the first four lines, McKay insists that the oppressed group of people to which he belongs not act like hogs, even though his oppressors have taken the part of "hungry dogs." In the seventh line, these dogs become "monsters," but by the final couplet they have returned to being a "murderous, cowardly pack." The speaker and his group, however, are on the verge of becoming heroic, ready to "deal one deathblow" for the "thousand blows" of their opponents.

If We Must Die

If we must die, let it not be like hogs
Hunted and penned in an inglorious spot,
While round us bark the mad and hungry dogs,
Making their mock at our accursed lot.
If we must die, O let us nobly die,
So that our precious blood may not be shed
In vain; then even the monsters we defy
Shall be constrained to honor us though dead!
O kinsmen! we must meet the common foe!
Though far outnumbered let us show us brave,
And for their thousand blows deal one deathblow!
What though before us lies the open grave?
Like men we'll face the murderous, cowardly pack,
Pressed to the wall, dying, but fighting back!

Claude McKay

Claude McKay's rebelliousness is grounded in a specific historical time and place. As an African-American man, he has personal knowledge of the sting of racism even if he was not present at the worst of the 1919 riots, which occurred in Chicago, where thirty-eight people were killed and more than one thousand African-American families were left homeless.

Jamie Molitor's poem, on the other hand, discusses a different sort of defiance altogether. Perhaps taking a cue from "If We Must Die," Jamie "becomes" an animal. Speaking from the point of view of not just one salmon but the entire species, he writes about the salmon's genetic imperative to swim upstream and spawn. The defiant aspect of this act is, of course, that the arduous trip is a prelude to the fish's own death. Thus the repeated line "Another year, another try" is both scientifically accurate—each year salmon swim in from the ocean to spawn—and bitterly ironic—for individual salmon there will be no more years and no more tries.

Both "If We Must Die" and "Salmon March" effectively employ **hyperbole** (hi-PER-bo-lee), that is, exaggerated or extravagant speech. An example can be seen in McKay's line "What though before us lies the open grave?" Here we are meant to understand that there is not, literally, an open grave in front of the oppressed group but rather the prospect of death. Likewise in Jamie's poem, while salmon certainly will have a hard time fighting their way upstream, they don't actually challenge a river "drip by drip." Nevertheless, seen within the contexts of the poems in which they appear, these overstatements are essential to creating a world where risks and rewards are magnified far beyond the everyday.

One word of caution: hyperbole can backfire when it is used carelessly. Take a sentence like "My stomach grumbled, rumbled, and exploded like the combined force of the U. S. nuclear arsenal when I went twenty minutes between candy bars." Unless this is meant to be comic, the writer has clearly used far more exaggeration than is necessary to make her point.

Salmon March

Each year we make this fateful trip.
  We challenge this river, drip by drip.
And up and up this way we go,
  A job to do, our seed to sow.
And up and up this way we fly,
  Another year, another try.

Until we reach our bitter end
  We swim and jump and flop and bend.
And up and up this way we go,
  A job to do, our seed to sow.
And up and up this way we fly,
  Another year, another try.

Jamie Molitor

Your Turn

Write your own poem that challenges a mighty opponent and asserts your strength or the strength of a group to which you belong. If you feel that you are not "in defiance" against anyone or anything, you are not alone. However, further thinking on the subject will probably reveal that there *are* mighty opponents you want to challenge.

Consider, for instance, the following topics generated by students who initially felt they could not complete this assignment: A member of the color guard (the corps that does tricks with flags while the marching band plays) derides the football team for looking down on her organization. A young man lashes out at his girlfriend's friends, who he feels are unfairly arrayed against him. A fast-food worker confronts his tyrannical boss. A new mother reprimands the women in her husband's family who insinuate that she doesn't know how to take care of her child.

Chapter Ten

Thinking Small

The poems in this chapter magnify small things so that they seem big. A dragonfly, a piece of bark—objects we would normally consider inconsequential—become the subject matter for poetry. Indeed, the motto for this chapter might actually be *Write Small, Think Big.*

In some form or another, this motto has been a part of poetry for a long time. Long before Europeans discovered America, Chinese poets like Li Po and Tu Fu—and, later, the great Japanese haiku poets Basho, Buson, and Issa—had shown that tiny poems with tiny subjects can be memorable. Whether they were writing about cicadas or sparrows, mosquitoes or fireflies or frogs, these masters knew that looking closely at a diminutive creature or object could shed light on much larger issues; they believed a perfect, precise image could convey volumes of information.

If you live in a place where dragonflies are common, you know how easy it is to ignore these

41

insects. By the end of summer you no longer pay attention to them, despite their monstrous appearance when seen up close. Yet their features *are* extraordinary. Their heads are huge in comparison to their long, thin thoraxes. Their compound eyes are like a space alien's. Their mouths are adapted for grabbing prey while in mid-flight. On reflection, the dragonfly turns out to be an excellent subject for a poem, if only someone would take the time to notice. Louise Bogan has.

The Dragonfly

You are made of almost nothing
But of enough
To be great eyes
And diaphanous double vans,
To be ceaseless movement,
Unending hunger
Grappling love.

Link between water and air,
Earth repels you.
Light touches you only to shift into iridescence
Upon your body and wings.

Twice-born, predator,
You split into the heat.
Swift beyond calculation or capture
You dart into the shadow
Which consumes you.

You rocket into the day.
But at last, when the wind flattens the grasses,
For you, the design and purpose stop.
And you fall
With the other husks of summer.

Louise Bogan

Different types of literature do different things well. Drama provides an opportunity to bring words to life, and it encourages collaboration between people with different ideas and talents. The personal essay creates a space for extended reflection. The novel is big enough to encompass the lives of many characters, to examine cultures, and to chart the course of history. The **lyric poem**—the category under which many of the poems in this book fall—is a brief poem that expresses a speaker's thoughts and emotions and does not attempt to tell a story.

Lyric poets prefer to concentrate intently on a single person, object, or emotion. Obviously, what the poet writes about does not necessarily have to be small, but there is a certain appropriateness in choosing a little subject for a little poem. Ironically, by keeping one's focus limited, it is possible to make some rather large statements.

Louise Bogan manages this feat in "The Dragonfly" by providing us with an accurate scientific description that remains open to a more mystical interpretation. Thus, in the first stanza we have a faithful depiction of the dragonfly's body, its feeding and mating habits. The second, third, and the first part of the fourth stanzas all show us what it looks like in flight, and the final lines tell us when its life cycle ends. Yet throughout the poem Bogan also idealizes the dragonfly. To take just one instance, rather than "see-through wings," Bogan uses the term "diaphanous double vans." The latter phrasing allows her the luxury of using an archaic word for wings, which may remind us that this creature that lives and dies in the course of a few months has been around since the dinosaurs.

Bogan's centerpiece is animate; Andy Johnson's is inanimate. Bogan's focus remains on her subject throughout; Andy's quickly shifts to himself and then his beloved. Nevertheless, Andy has followed the spirit of the assignment. The object that engenders his poem is small: a piece of bark. As the poem begins, he is bent over it, kneeling in the grass. Despite the obstacles presented by Nature—the starling chirping its disdain, the "thick, vengeful raindrops," the relentless sun—the speaker concentrates all his energy on carving his girlfriend's name into the modest space available for such a task. Yet, paradoxically, by focusing his attention on something so diminutive, he hopes that when he is finished, "Nature shall announce [the woman's] name / In company with itself."

I'm kneeling in the grass, carving into the bark.
The starling chirps its disdain.

Carving   I feel thick, vengeful raindrops
But I press on, carving, carefully carving.

The sun relentlessly burns my patient back
As it glides away unwillingly to submit to night.

I'll carve on, my love,
Though the night is black.

Nature shall announce your name
In company with itself,
For its beauty is matched by you.

Andrew Johnson

Your Turn

Write a poem in which you make something small seem grand. While you may have to do some exaggerating, as Bogan and Andy do, try to make sure your overstatement is appropriate to whatever you write about.

If a subject for this assignment does not come immediately to mind, remember that you have plenty of leeway to decide just what "small" is. You are thinking small if the subject of your poem is little *in relation to* whatever it is compared with.

Chapter Eleven

Urban Landmarks

This chapter asks you to write a poem addressed to an urban landmark. Whether it be a well-known structure like the Brooklyn Bridge or St. Louis's Gateway Arch (the subject of the two poems below), or something of lesser renown, the urban landmark you discuss should inspire in you an emotion beyond the ordinary.

My experience with the model poem in this chapter, Hart Crane's "To Brooklyn Bridge," has been that while most literary critics love it, students are initially bewildered. I think that is because literary critics, who have already read and absorbed thousands of poems, respond enthusiastically to the very thing that frustrates students: Crane's elaborate, sometimes frenzied language.

It is worth knowing, first of all, that "To Brooklyn Bridge" is the opening poem in Crane's book-length series, *The Bridge.* For Crane, the bridge was a symbol of "transition"; it was "an act of faith" and "a communication." In fact, he sees it as an object that is every bit as worthy of admiration as, say, the Roman Colosseum or the Great Pyramids of Egypt. (This reverence tempts him into using archaic words like *guerdon,* which means *reward,* and *Thee* and *Thy* whenever he directly addresses the bridge.)

To Brooklyn Bridge

How many dawns, chill from his rippling rest
The seagull's wings shall dip and pivot him,
Shedding white rings of tumult, building high
Over the chained bay waters Liberty—

Then, with inviolate curve, forsake our eyes
As apparitional as sails that cross
Some page of figures to be filed away;
—Till elevators drop us from our day . . .

I think of cinemas, panoramic sleights
With multitudes bent toward some flashing scene
Never disclosed, but hastened to again,
Foretold to other eyes on the same screen;

And Thee, across the harbor, silver-paced
As though the sun took step of thee, yet left
Some motion ever unspent in thy stride,—
Implicitly thy freedom staying thee!

Out of some subway scuttle, cell or loft
A bedlamite speeds to thy parapets,
Tilting there momently, shrill shirt ballooning,
A jest falls from the speechless caravan.

Down Wall, from girder into street noon leaks,
A rip-tooth of the sky's acetylene;
All afternoon the cloud-flown derricks turn . . .
Thy cables breathe the North Atlantic still.

And obscure as that heaven of the Jews,
Thy guerdon . . . Accolade thou dost bestow
Of anonymity time cannot raise:
Vibrant reprieve and pardon thou dost show.

O harp and altar, of the fury fused,
(How could mere toil align thy choiring strings!)

Terrific threshold of the prophet's pledge,
Prayer of pariah, and the lover's cry,—

Again the traffic lights that skim thy swift
Unfractioned idiom, immaculate sigh of stars,
Beading thy path—condense eternity:
And we have seen night lifted in thine arms.

Under thy shadow by the piers I waited;
Only in darkness is thy shadow clear.
The City's fiery parcels all undone,
Already snow submerges an iron year . . .

O Sleepless as the river under thee,
Vaulting the sea, the prairies' dreaming sod,
Unto us lowliest sometime sweep, descend
And of the curveship lend a myth to God.

Hart Crane

Crane's is a style that takes some getting used to. Until you feel comfortable with his eccentric syntax and surrealistic leaps of thought, it may be best to think of this complicated poem as a kind of early twentieth-century precursor to the music video. (In fact, two series that have appeared on PBS, *Voices and Visions* [which includes a feature on Crane] and *The United States of Poetry*, have, for better or worse, managed to MTV-ize contemporary American poetry.) Now that you have read the poem, imagine how a contemporary videographer might approach its random sequences and jump cuts (EXT. and INT. are abbreviations for exterior and interior):

EXT. NEW YORK CITY
Camera follows a seagull making its way from the Statue of Liberty toward the city.

NEW ANGLE—NYC
The gull glides past the Brooklyn Bridge.

INT. MOVIE HOUSE
People staring at the screen, some leaning forward. All engrossed.

EXT. BROOKLYN BRIDGE
Sun shining on the bridge's cables.

EXT. STREET SCENE
People pouring from a subway entrance.

EXT. NEW YORK BROWNSTONE
A man dressed for work leaves his building.

EXT. BROOKLYN BRIDGE
Rush hour crowds converge on the bridge.

EXT. SKYSCRAPER UNDER CONSTRUCTION
Several workers welding steel. Dissolve to

EXT. BROOKLYN BRIDGE
Clouds pass over the bridge. Camera pans upward, toward "the heaven of the Jews."

MONTAGE
The following images swirl into one another: Clouds, a bearded man playing a harp, the bridge's cables, traffic lights, a field of stars, a man lifting his arms before he is enveloped by blackness.

EXT. BROOKLYN BRIDGE—NIGHT
A man stands under the bridge in the shadows as snow falls. Camera pans to the river, follows the line of the bridge westward. Dissolve to

EXT. PRAIRIE
An aerial shot, emphasizing wind on the tall grass, the vastness of the Midwest. Dissolve to

EXT. BROOKLYN BRIDGE
Sunlight sparkling on the gleaming, curving cables of the bridge.

BLACKOUT

If you have trouble understanding "To Brooklyn Bridge," part of the reason might be Crane's unusual manipulation of diction and syntax. **Diction** refers to a writer's choice of words, phrases, sentence structure, and figurative language. **Syntax** is the way in which words or phrases are combined to form a sentence.

Obviously, there are different types of diction. In everyday conversation, we tend to use **informal diction.** When you write a term paper for class, you are likely to avoid contractions, make certain there are no fragments or run-on sentences, and so on—in short, you employ a much more **formal diction.** The term **poetic diction,** which certainly applies to Crane's poem, alludes to the sort of elevated speech that would sound ridiculous in ordinary conversation. Over the course of the twentieth century, the term has come to have mostly pejorative connotations, and creative writing teachers usually advise their students to write poems that sound like someone talking to a friend, not a Shakespearean hero or heroine delivering a soliloquy.

Just as we are used to hearing and reading a certain type of diction, we are also used to standard syntax, in which the subject, verb, and complement come in a predictable order. Sarah Brown's poem adheres to these expectations, but Crane's definitely does not. To take just one example, look at the first two lines of stanza six: "Down Wall, from girder into street noon leaks, / A rip-tooth of the sky's acetylene." A more comprehensible paraphrase would read: "Noon leaks, like a rip-tooth of the sky's acetylene, down Wall Street, from girder to street level." We would expect to see the prepositional phrases "Down Wall [Street]" and "from girder to street [level]" after the subject and verb, rather than before. But Crane twists everything around, forcing us to abandon our normal ways of reading, in which we tend to glide over words without directly confronting them. Instead, we must make sense of his poem piece by piece. Whether or not this aesthetic is to your taste, it is certainly effective in making the average reader say, "Whoa!"

Of course a poem addressed to an urban landmark does not have to strain the limits of our comprehension. Where Hart Crane pushes his sentences to the edge of chaos, Sarah Brown strives for clarity. Her poem describes what it is like to approach the Gateway Arch in St. Louis from Illinois. A 630-foot ribbon of stainless steel, the Arch towers over the city's skyline and, as Sarah notes, is meant to serve as a focal point for travelers crossing the Mississippi River from the east to the west. Ironically, Sarah reveals, once this passage is made, the Arch loses much of its luster, becoming "Plain, / dull metal rapidly receding as / we sink into St. Louis."

Arch

Through the labyrinth
of overpasses, underpasses, bypasses;
of asphalt ribbons leading like a 3-D
filigree bridge to this central point,
I see you slowly emerging from the haze
of smog, smoke and fickle
Midwestern heat clouds.
A shining silver gate to the larger states
of horses, wheat and slowed-down speech,
you step out from the mists, growing
larger and larger, expanding to a full reality
that I could possibly grab from my 55 mile
an hour car window. The sun reflects off
your smooth, metal sheet plates in blinding,
widening points. Larger, brighter,

brilliant holy light merging closer and closer into
One
column as we pass and your
other side is revealed. Plain,
dull metal rapidly receding as
we sink into St. Louis.

Sarah Brown

Your Turn

Choose an urban landmark and address a poem to it. If you set your poem in America, you might choose the Empire State Building, the Golden Gate Bridge, the Washington or Lincoln Monument, or the Astrodome. A poem set in Paris might be about
Notre Dame Cathedral or the Eiffel Tower or the Arc de Triomphe. A London setting
might inspire a poem to Saint Paul's Cathedral or the Tower of London or Big Ben,
and so on.

    You may, however, want to focus on an urban landmark smaller and closer to
home. The World War I cannon in the town square, the clock atop city hall, even the
statue of a local hero could make a suitable topic and might well generate an outstanding poem.

Chapter Twelve

Shadow of the Blues

Jazz musicians often say that even when they are playing at their freest, there is still, somewhere at the core of their music, a hint of the basic blues structure from which jazz was born. In this chapter you will be writing a poem that has a similar relationship to a type of music you admire. Although it will not be set to any melody, your poem should nevertheless have musical qualities or suggest a certain type of music.

In Langston Hughes's *Selected Poems,* "The Weary Blues" is included in a section entitled "Shadow of the Blues." Although the poem quotes several blues stanzas, it does, indeed, seem more like a shadow of the blues than a blues lyric. In fact, the only part of the poem that actually fits into the twelve-bar blues form is the final indented section in quotation marks.

Yet if the poem does not rigorously adhere to the original model, there is no doubt that Hughes takes advantage of the blues to create a suitable *atmosphere* for his description of an African-American singer in a Harlem nightclub. In addition to the blues lyrics, Hughes employs other, more traditional, poetic devices. He uses the **refrain**—a phrase repeated at intervals—"O Blues!" and its variation "Sweet Blues!" And **rhyming couplets,** pairs of lines that rhyme and have the same meter, are found throughout the poem. Taken together, this insistence on rhythm and rhyme make "The Weary Blues" about as close to a piece of music as it is possible to get without a band playing in the background.

The Weary Blues

Droning a drowsy syncopated tune,
Rocking back and forth to a mellow croon,
    I heard a Negro play.
Down on Lenox Avenue the other night
By the pale dull pallor of an old gas light
    He did a lazy sway . . . .
    He did a lazy sway . . . .
To the tune o' those Weary Blues.
With his ebony hands on each ivory key
He made that poor piano moan with melody.
    O Blues!
Swaying to and fro on his rickety stool
He played that sad raggy tune like a musical fool.
    Sweet Blues!
Coming from a black man's soul.
    O Blues!
In a deep song voice with a melancholy tone
I heard that Negro sing, that old piano moan—
    "Ain't got nobody in all this world,
    Ain't got nobody but ma self.
    I's gwine to quit ma frownin'
    And put ma troubles on the shelf."

Thump, thump, thump, went his foot on the floor.
He played a few chords then he sang some more—
    "I got the Weary Blues
    And I can't be satisfied
    Got the Weary Blues
    And can't be satisfied—
    I ain't happy no mo'
    And I wish that I had died."
And far into the night he crooned that tune.
The stars went out and so did the moon.
The singer stopped playing and went to bed

While the Weary Blues echoed through his head.
He slept like a rock or a man that's dead.

Langston Hughes

Dialect is a type of language unique to a specific regional or social group. Examples in "The Weary Blues" include "ma self" for "myself" and "gwine" for "going." While dialect is far more likely to be used in a story or a novel, poets occasionally find dialect—with its inventive variations on standard speech—a rich source for their poetry. For Langston Hughes, dialect was often a means of incorporating the authentic language of the people around him, a language that, in the early part of this century, was not likely to find itself in serious literature.

Be careful, though. If you are not a member of the group who normally speaks the dialect, you may come off sounding condescending or just plain silly. (Compare, for instance, "The Weary Blues" with the novel and the lyrics of the opera *Porgy and Bess,* written by DuBose Heyward, a white man.) As a general rule, it is probably best to avoid dialect unless you are intimately familiar with it.

Sometimes called a "blues poet," Langston Hughes wrote from within a particular cultural legacy. Jackie Mitchell's "Costa Rican Jump Rope Love Song," on the other hand, is both inside and outside a tradition. Jackie's poem taps into a familiar musical form, albeit a very informal one: the jump rope song. A former jump-roper herself, Jackie was well-acquainted with many of the songs American children use to help them keep time. However, the idea for the poem came while Jackie was in Costa Rica, a place she had never been before. She watched and took notes as three children jumped rope in a San José alley. Their song was in Spanish, and the words were entirely different from the songs of her youth, but the scene fused with Jackie's childhood memories to produce a fine poem.

A perfectionist, Jackie actually jump-roped to the poem to make sure the beats were compatible with this rhythmic physical activity. (Note: Hector is pronounced *EK-tor* and Adriana is *ah-dree-AH-nuh*.)

Costa Rican Jump Rope Love Song

Hector, Hector
loved his Adriana.
Hector, he told her
he'd do anything she wanted,
cause she'd spin
like a whirlwind,
a dust devil dancing when
he'd strum his guitar
'neath the Costa Rican sun.

Hector, Hector
loved his Adriana.
Hector, he gave her
a sun-splashing demon
cause she'd canter in amber sand,
tossing shells in handfuls and
sing to calm the centaurs
of the Costa Rican sun.

Hector, Hector
loved his Adriana.
Hector, he twirled her
like a galaxy, a nova
and they'd spin
to the ends
of where time and light begins.
A spark-shooting star,
they are Costa Rican sun.

Count their sunrays.
Start with one.

One . . . Two . . . Three . . . Four . . .

Jackie Mitchell

Your Turn

Use some form of music you enjoy to help you structure a poem about that type of music. Langston Hughes writes about the blues. Jackie Mitchell riffs on jump-rope songs. You may find your ideal musical form is a waltz, a hymn, a rock song, or even a polka.

Do not assume that your poem has to take the form of a song lyric. Rather than penning the words to a samba, for instance, you might instead try to write a poem that is as syncopated and percussive as the samba itself. Or your poem might be about participation in your church choir. Your poem may not make a good hymn, but it should describe and "echo" hymn singing in a way that allows your reader to become part of that sometimes solemn, sometimes joyful experience.

Chapter Thirteen

Confronting Prejudice

The subject of this chapter's poems is racial prejudice. Your own poem may well feature a head-on confrontation, one in which the participants exchange words, or even blows. It is worth noting, however, that neither the model poem nor the student response focuses on a full-scale conflict. There are no riots, no burning crosses. Instead, these poems show bigotry taking more subtle, if still very hurtful, forms.

Before you begin reading or writing, though, we should acknowledge that race is a touchy subject. Whether we interact daily with people of other races, or rarely do so at all, we are aware that resentment and suspicions may boil over at even the most unexpected times. Because we realize that a frank discussion of racial problems in our country can mean trouble, we tend to avoid such discussions.

Yet some of the most powerful American poets have tackled the subject. In Countee Cullen's "Incident," a painful childhood memory becomes the subject of an unforgettable poem. The speaker, too young to know anything about prejudice, visits a large Southern city. When he smiles at a boy his own age, his gesture of friendliness is met with contempt. The boy's curt insult reverberates throughout the speaker's visit and, indeed, throughout his life.

Cullen's skillful use of plain language results in the sort of poem one readily commits to memory. He is also aided by the use of perfect rhymes, which emphasize the links between sound and sense. "[B]igger" - "Nigger" and "December" - "remember," especially, burn themselves into our consciousness.

Incident

For Eric Walrond

Once riding in old Baltimore,
    Heart-filled, head-filled with glee,
I saw a Baltimorean
    Keep looking straight at me.

Now I was eight and very small,
    And he was no whit bigger,
And so I smiled, but he poked out
    His tongue, and called me, "Nigger."

I saw the whole of Baltimore
    From May until December;
Of all the things that happened there
    That's all that I remember.

Countee Cullen

Cullen's poem is a very elegant, some would say a very *traditional* piece of writing. An African-American poet addressing a racially charged incident, he nevertheless avoids the racial dialect found in Langston Hughes's "The Weary Blues." Of course, it would be foolish to expect poets to write in a particular style simply because of their race or gender or any other factor. Nevertheless, there does seem to be a certain intentional irony in the fact that Cullen's control of language shows him to be far superior to the type of person who is likely to spit out a racial slur on a streetcorner.

In contrast with "Incident," Kelly Janssen's "Natural" is written from the point of view of a member of the racial majority. A bystander to the main action of the poem, Kelly could conceivably keep a psychic distance between herself and the instance of prejudice she sees: her grandfather's racist assumption about the young woman leaving his grandson's apartment. Yet the incident clearly does bother her; otherwise the poem would not exist.

In just a few lines, Kelly manages to introduce a complex set of relationships. While he is the one who utters the disparaging remark, the grandfather may not be entirely at fault. After all, Vivica does not stop to introduce herself, and Rob makes no attempt to introduce her to his family as his girlfriend. Perhaps the couple fear what Rob's family will say, but we never find out. Kelly leaves us guessing about the intricate family and cultural dynamics that have preceded and will ensue from this brief scene.

Despite the different poetic approaches, however, there is clearly a kinship between the two poems. Neither flinches from a frank description of racial conflict. Neither makes apologies for the ugliness. Both twist the knife at the very end with an unexpected concluding line. Yet both make possible the beginning of a dialogue about racism. In fact, Kelly seems to be investigating the very sources of prejudice that would produce a remark like the one that was so wounding to Countee Cullen.

In the last fifteen or twenty years, student poems like Kelly's, which confront the causes and effects of racial prejudice, have become much more common. In part, this may be due to the civil rights struggles of the 1950s and 1960s. These struggles engendered a "movement" that has become known as **multiculturalism.** Everything from politics to poetry has been touched by multiculturalism, and there are probably as many definitions for this term as there are multiculturalists. One way of looking at it is to say that, from this perspective, an ideal society is one that includes the ideas and opinions of as diverse a group of women and men as possible. Multiculturalists often feel that in America only one side has been adequately represented: that of white males with political and economic power. Their goal is to ensure that other voices, like those of Countee Cullen and Vivica in Kelly's poem, are given a fair and equal hearing.

Interestingly, had the term been around then, Cullen might not have considered himself a multiculturalist. Of Langston Hughes's collection *The Weary Blues,* he wrote: "Taken as a group the selections in this book seem one-sided to me. They tend to hurl this poet into the gaping pit that lies before all Negro writers, in the confines of which they become racial artists instead of artists pure and simple." This statement merits some thought: many people would argue that the relationship between art that celebrates the artist's racial identity and art "pure and simple" is probably more complicated than Cullen implies. Some poets, like Langston Hughes, might say that the two are indivisible. In any case, multiculturalists would tell us it is a topic worth discussing, and your class might want to do just that.

Natural

A young Filipino girl
dressed in khaki shorts
and a plain white T-shirt
opened the front door
and brushed past my grandfather.

"See you tomorrow, Rob,"
she called out, forgetting
to close the gate as she left.

"Damn cleaning ladies.
Never even say, 'Excuse me,'"
Grandpa muttered as we entered
my brother's apartment.

Mom ignored him,
Dad agreed;
Rob didn't utter
a single word.

I asked,
"Wasn't that Vivica,
your girlfriend?"

Kelly Janssen

Your Turn

Write a poem that illustrates an example of racial prejudice. Remember, though, that you are not writing an essay. In other words, don't feel as if you have to come to some definitive conclusion about the subject, or even that you need to formulate all the important questions. Like "Incident" and "Natural," your poem should focus on a specific occasion, one that will resonate for both you and your readers.

This topic may call forth the orator in you, but fight the urge to be melodramatic. Granted, poetry uses more eloquent language than we normally require, but if you started speaking to your friends the way you are speaking in your poem, would you be embarrassed? Let the incident you describe provide your commentary for you.

Chapter Fourteen

Conditional Love

The theme of this chapter is love, but with a difference. While you will not exactly be writing an *anti*love poem, you will be substantially modifying the conventions. The sample poems (and the poem that you will write) admit love is not perfect. They go beyond the timeworn sentiment of "You are ideal in every way," and instead concede that "While I do love you, you are human and therefore of necessity flawed."

Common sense tells us that this is hardly an outlandish admission, but our experience as readers insists that love poetry should never reveal any of the beloved's blemishes. Usually when people are moved enough to write love poems, they feel no compunction about exaggerating their dear one's many virtues. W. H. Auden argues against this all-or-nothing thinking. He writes in a mode that most lovers would prefer to ignore, although it is not a mode without a tradition. "Lullaby" may even have been intended as a twentieth-century updating of Shakespeare's "My Mistress' Eyes Are Nothing Like the Sun." That sonnet, you will remember, begins: "My mistress' eyes are nothing like the sun; / Coral is far more red than her lips' red; / If snow be white, why then her breasts are dun; / If hairs be wires, black wires grow on her head."

Auden's poem, however, is less comical and more complex than Shakespeare's. The speaker of "Lullaby" acknowledges that the arm holding his beloved is "faithless," and he realizes that his lover is both "Mortal" and "guilty." The opening lines of the third stanza—"Certainty, fidelity / On the stroke of midnight pass / Like vibrations of a bell"—evoke the story of Cinderella. Yet, unlike the fairy tale, Auden's poem argues that no happy-ever-after will follow. The lovers will have to be content with the time they spend together, for the future holds nothing but trouble: "Every farthing of the cost, / All the dreaded cards foretell, / Shall be paid." (*Note:* The text below is that of the 1937 version of the poem.)

Lullaby

Lay your sleeping head, my love,
Human on my faithless arm;
Time and fevers burn away
Individual beauty from
Thoughtful children, and the grave
Proves the child ephemeral:
But in my arms till break of day
Let the living creature lie,
Mortal, guilty, but to me
The entirely beautiful.

Soul and body have no bounds:
To lovers as they lie upon
Her tolerant enchanted slope
In their ordinary swoon,
Grave the vision Venus sends
Of supernatural sympathy,
Universal love and hope;
While an abstract insight wakes
Among the glaciers and the rocks
The hermit's sensual ecstasy.

Certainty, fidelity
On the stroke of midnight pass
Like vibrations of a bell,
And fashionable madmen raise
Their pedantic boring cry:
Every farthing of the cost,

All the dreaded cards foretell,
Shall be paid, but from this night
Not a whisper, not a thought,
Not a kiss nor look be lost.

Beauty, midnight, vision dies:
Let the winds of dawn that blow
Softly round your dreaming head
Such a day of sweetness show
Eye and knocking heart may bless,
Find the mortal world enough;
Noons of dryness see you fed
By the involuntary powers,
Nights of insult let you pass
Watched by every human love.

W. H. Auden

One of the ways that Auden evokes a mood in which every pure, romantic notion seems to be immediately undercut by harsh and skeptical reality is through his use of adjectives. At crucial points in the poem, nouns that we would expect to have one sort of modifier turn out to have another type altogether. In the second stanza, for instance, he describes the condition of being in love as an "ordinary swoon," thus robbing it of any special qualities. Then he refers to "The hermit's sensual ecstasy." Hermits, whom we typically associate with spirituality (a hermitage is a monastery or an abbey), are, in Auden's universe, as carnal as the rest of us. Perhaps that is because, as he states in the final stanza, the "powers" of the world are "involuntary." They surge automatically through saint and sinner alike.

Pam Dwyer's poem "To Lloyd" uses simpler, more direct language to achieve some of the same ends as Auden's lullaby. The speaker has recently come to see some of the flaws in her boyfriend that she never noticed before: he seems physically less appealing, and she has questions about his faithfulness. She claims that she probably still loves him—he's handsome and "give[s] good gossip"—but she now wonders if their relationship has ever been everything she once thought it was.

Pam divides her poem into three-line stanzas called **tercets.** Like a snapshot or a miniature painting, each tercet presents a picture of the speaker's relationship with Lloyd. The opening and closing stanzas are meditations on the relationship, but the other five are, truly, "pictures" of Lloyd: combing his hair, brushing his teeth, winking at the speaker's friend, and so on. Rather than trying to explain the entire relationship, Pam has wisely chosen to show a few select, revealing moments. This method allows her readers to gain specific insights into Lloyd's character while leaving a great deal open to our imaginations.

To Lloyd

I'm not sure when
I realized
you weren't perfect.

Maybe it was the first
morning I saw you
with your hair uncombed,

or smelled your breath
before you'd washed
your teeth with peppermint.

It could have been
the afternoon I caught you
winking at my best friend,

or that night I saw you
outside Burger King
with your "ex-" girlfriend.

I guess I love you still.
You're handsome.
You give good gossip.

But things aren't perfect
between us anymore—
if they ever were.

Pam Dwyer

Your Turn

Write a love poem in which you, too, concede that love, though "entirely beautiful," is nevertheless "human" and maybe even "faithless." The poem may refer to your beloved in the third person or, like Auden and Pam, you may address him or her directly. Be especially vigilant of clichés. Even in an assignment designed to discourage them, clichés have an insidious way of working themselves into love poetry.

If you have just fallen in love, or if you are of a particularly romantic turn of mind, this poem may be difficult to write. As you sit at your computer gazing across the room at your beloved, you may find it impossible to believe that anything could be "human" about that god or goddess—much less "faithless"!

Should that be the case (or if you happen to be alone right now), you may want to invent a lover. Even though this person is imaginary, it will help if he or she seems real. Therefore, take some time to jot down the person's characteristics, both good and bad. How old is he or she? Where was the person born? Now shut your eyes. Give him or her a face and a body (it is okay to borrow one from someone you know). When your fictitious beloved begins to take shape, start writing.

Chapter Fifteen

Elegies

In this chapter, you will write an **elegy,** that is, a
lament for a particular person's death. Your poem
should mark the passing of a person who has in
some significant way affected your life. For Greek
and Latin poets, the term *elegy* had more to do with
the type of stanzas in the poem than it did with the
subject matter. And up until the sixteenth century,
the subject of an elegy could be any number of
things, but especially romantic love. During the
seventeenth century, however, *elegy* began to take on
the meaning it has today: a mournful poem,
especially one grieving for someone who has died.

Some of the more famous elegies in English are
John Milton's "Lycidas," Percy Bysshe Shelley's
"Thyrsis," Alfred Tennyson's *In Memoriam A.H.H.*
("'T is better to have loved and lost / Than never to
have loved at all,"), Walt Whitman's "When Lilacs
Last in the Dooryard Bloom'd" and W. H. Auden's
"In Memory of W. B. Yeats." All these poems use a
specific person's passing to mediate on the larger
subject of death and its twin, life. Inevitably, poems

like "Elegy for Jane" by Theodore Roethke (pronounced RET-key) and "When I Think of Daddy" by Taneeka Jackson tell us as much, if not more, about the speaker as they do about the person who is gone.

Roethke's "Elegy for Jane" is widely considered one of his most moving poems although, ironically, the subject of the elegy is a student Roethke did not know well. In the absence of biographical details he relies heavily on metaphorical language ("pickerel smile," "my wren," "my skittery pigeon") to make Jane more vivid to his reader. She was thrown by a horse, and Roethke repeatedly compares her with other animals, insisting that even the plant kingdom was sympathetic to her: "Her song trembling the twigs and small branches. / The shade sang with her; / The leaves, their whispers turned to kissing."

Indeed, the poet seems to find some relief from his sorrow by emphasizing Jane's connection with the natural world while she was alive. It is almost as though because she lived in closer harmony with the earth and its creatures than most of us do, the transition into a less sentient state will be easier for her. In any case, Roethke's distance from the person he is memorializing does not preclude him from writing with passion and insight on the subject of death.

Elegy for Jane
My Student, Thrown by a Horse

I remember the neckcurls, limp and damp as tendrils;
And her quick look, a sidelong pickerel smile;
And how, once startled into talk, the light syllables leaped for her,
And she balanced in the delight of her thought,
A wren, happy, tail into the wind,
Her song trembling the twigs and small branches.
The shade sang with her;
The leaves, their whispers turned to kissing;
And the mold sang in the bleached valleys under the rose.

Oh, when she was sad, she cast herself down into such a
    pure depth,
Even a father could not find her:
Scraping her cheek against straw;
Stirring the clearest water.

 My sparrow, you are not here,
Waiting like a fern, making a spiny shadow.
The sides of wet stones cannot console me,
Nor the moss, wound with the last light.

If only I could nudge you from this sleep,
My maimed darling, my skittery pigeon.
Over this damp grave I speak the words of my love:
I, with no rights in this matter,
Neither father nor lover.

Theodore Roethke

A somber poem like an elegy would seem to require somber imagery, and Roethke provides it in plenty. The air is damp; leaves whisper in the shade; moss grows beside wet stones; it is twilight; a man stands over a freshly dug grave. Fortunately, Roethke introduces this imagery in a highly inventive way. He does not, for instance, simply say that mold is spreading under the roses. Instead, he writes: "And the mold sang in the bleached valleys under the rose." In addition to providing us with the dreary picture of a bleached valley, the poet gives us singing mold. The act of endowing an abstraction or an object that is inanimate (or barely animate, like mold) with living characteristics or with human attributes and feelings is called **personification.** (Incidentally, it is precisely because poets so often personify things that poetry can seem so strange to novice readers.)

Theodore Roethke not only has a clever way with phrasing, he also has a terrific ear for the "music" of poetry, the way its sounds harmonize with one another. Two of the most common devices used to incorporate music into a poem are alliteration and assonance. **Alliteration** is the repetition of consonant sounds in nearby words—the "*s*" sounds, for instance, in line eight: "leav*es*," "whisper*s*," "ki*ss*ing." **Assonance** is the repetition of internal vowel sounds, as in "s*a*d" and "c*a*st" in line ten.

Taneeka Jackson is another poet with a good ear for music, though the imagery in her poem is much livelier, much more contemporary than Roethke's. Of "When I Think of Daddy," Taneeka writes: "My father died before my eighteenth birthday; he lost his battle with cancer. Being your typical daddy's girl, and never having lost a loved one so close to me, I suffered through many years of depression. My father was my role model, and after his death I inadvertently took on many of his characteristics. Writing this poem helped me to put into words what my heart was feeling."

Like Roethke, Taneeka relies on specific details to explain her relationship with her father. She discusses what he liked to eat and drink, how he drove his car, his religious convictions, even what he watched on TV. Moreover, because Taneeka has been moved to emulate him since his death, we learn about both father *and* daughter in her poem.

For Taneeka, again like Roethke, the elegy provides an opportunity to move past grief. Both poets seek to understand and find consolation in a loved one's death through the writing of difficult, but ultimately cathartic, poems.

When I Think of Daddy

When I think of Daddy
I eat black-eyed peas and rice
Fire up a Marlboro
Drink Reunite on ice
    Never could stomach the taste of beer

When I think of Daddy
I drive down the street with a gangsta lean
Nodding and waving
I go to a stranger and do something nice
    Never having to be asked for a favor

When I think of Daddy
I search the mirror for his face
Tell a funny joke or stare
I place my hands in the brim of my pants
Watch "Murder She Wrote" or "Matlock"
    Why do they always win?

When I think of Daddy
I read the Good Book
Say a solemn prayer
Remove the phone
Hold my breath and count to ten
    Sometimes I don't feel like crying

I think of Daddy
Whatever it takes to bring him back
Even for a moment

Taneeka K. Jackson

Your Turn

Write an elegy. If possible, the poem should be about someone you knew, though you may not have known that person well. Remember that there is a difference between a eulogy and an elegy. The former is typically spoken at a memorial service and, as its prefix "eu-" (the Greek word for "well" or "good") suggests, is laudatory and full of praise. An elegy, on the other hand, is as much (or more) concerned with the *poetry* used to mourn the deceased person as it is with the actual person.

If you have never known anyone who has died, imagine what it would be like if someone close to you passed away. What specific events associated with that person would you want to recall in a literary memorial? What one or two characteristics about the person would you remember most? How would the person's death affect you? How would it affect others?

Chapter Sixteen

Should We Have Stayed at Home?

When you travel, you extricate yourself from your ordinary life. You see things that may amaze or delight you. You open yourself to insights that might otherwise never have occurred to you. Yet traveling can also involve discomfort and fatigue. It can frighten and disturb. Elizabeth Bishop and Vicki Brown Johnston have faced these issues. The speakers in their poems wonder aloud whether it is better to venture out or to remain safely at home. Your poem for this chapter will address that conundrum, too.

A compulsive traveler, Elizabeth Bishop spent much of her life writing about the pleasures and the sorrows of, as she puts it in "Questions of Travel," seeing "the sun the other way around." This complexity of emotional response makes her travel poetry successful on several levels. "Questions of Travel" presents a very clear travelogue of the author's adopted home, Brazil. "[T]he pressure of so many clouds on the mountaintops / makes them spill over the sides in soft slow-motion, / turning to waterfalls under our very eyes," she writes in the opening stanza, perfectly describing the illusion that a mass of clouds can turn into a waterfall. That same knack for description appears again toward the end of the poem when she depicts rain as "so much like politician's speeches, / two hours of unrelenting oratory / and then a sudden golden silence."

Without being ponderous, "Questions of Travel" also manages to raise some very philosophical questions. "Should we have stayed at home and thought of here?" she asks. And later, in a more self-deprecating tone: *"Is it lack of imagination that makes us come / to imagined places, not just stay at home?"* The answer to both questions is yes and no. Indeed, Bishop's poem is so effective, in part, because she creates a tension between her joy in seeing so many wonderful things and her guilt in having to come so far to view them. Her final admission that *"the choice is never wide and never free"* adds yet another note of poignancy to the entire meditation.

Questions of Travel

There are too many waterfalls here; the crowded streams
hurry too rapidly down to the sea,
and the pressure of so many clouds on the mountaintops
makes them spill over the sides in soft slow-motion,
turning to waterfalls under our very eyes.
—For if those streaks, those mile-long, shiny, tearstains,
aren't waterfalls yet,
in a quick age or so, as ages go here,
they probably will be.
But if the streams and clouds keep travelling, travelling,
the mountains look like the hulls of capsized ships,
slime-hung and barnacled.

Think of the long trip home.
Should we have stayed at home and thought of here?
Where should we be today?
Is it right to be watching strangers in a play
in this strangest of theatres?
What childishness is it that while there's a breath of life
in our bodies, we are determined to rush
to see the sun the other way around?
The tiniest green hummingbird in the world?
To stare at some inexplicable old stonework,
inexplicable and impenetrable,
at any view,
instantly seen and always, always delightful?
Oh, must we dream our dreams
and have them, too?

And have we room
for one more folded sunset, still quite warm?

But surely it would have been a pity
not to have seen the trees along this road,
really exaggerated in their beauty,
not to have seen them gesturing
like noble pantomimists, robed in pink.
—Not to have had to stop for gas and heard
the sad, two-noted, wooden tune
of disparate wooden clogs
carelessly clacking over
a grease-stained filling-station floor.
(In another country the clogs would all be tested.
Each pair there would have identical pitch.)
—A pity not to have heard
the other, less primitive music of the fat brown bird
who sings above the broken gasoline pump
in a bamboo church of Jesuit baroque:
three towers, five silver crosses.
—Yes, a pity not to have pondered,
blurr'dly and inconclusively,
on what connection can exist for centuries
between the crudest wooden footwear
and, careful and finicky,
the whittled fantasies of wooden cages.
—Never to have studied history in
the weak calligraphy of songbirds' cages.
—And never to have had to listen to rain
so much like politicians' speeches:
two hours of unrelenting oratory
and then a sudden golden silence
in which the traveller takes a notebook, writes:

"Is it lack of imagination that makes us come
to imagined places, not just stay at home?
Or could Pascal have been not entirely right
about just sitting quietly in one's room?

Continent, city, country, society:
the choice is never wide and never free.
And here, or there . . . No. Should we have stayed at home,
wherever that may be?"

Elizabeth Bishop

The best travel writing, whether it takes the form of poetry or prose, evokes sensory details that will help the reader transport herself to another place. In "Questions of Travel," Elizabeth Bishop appeals throughout not only to our sense of sight, but also to our sense of sound. There is "the sad, two-noted, wooden tune / of disparate wooden clogs / carelessly clacking over / a grease-stained filling-station floor." And "the other, less primitive music of the fat brown bird / who sings above the broken gasoline pump." The songs of the clogs and the bird, like the music of Bishop's poem, may be imperfect, but they are lovely nonetheless.

Vicki Brown Johnston is even more insistent on putting her reader in the picture. She is especially good at making us *feel* what she has felt, whether it be the unpleasant "sea-sickening pitch and rolls of the Atlantic Ocean wave-train," or the much more enjoyable sensation of skin being "covered by an undulating layer of white / butterflies" or soothed by "the homely joy of taking salt-free showers."

Vicki begins "Canegarden Bay, Tortola," in direct homage to the older poet by slightly rephrasing Bishop's first line. She then goes on to give a vivid description of sailing through the Caribbean. The noisy, sleepless, seasick nights intertwine with the many delights she experienced. Although she is writing years after taking the trip, Vicki says that "the sensory details even after all this time are still ingrained in my mind, and I can, to paraphrase Mark Twain writing of Hawaii, still smell the flowers which died long ago."

"Canegarden Bay" is such a memorable poem because it is so specific and because, while the trip was primarily an enjoyable one, the poet tells the other side of the story as well. By providing us with a spectrum of emotions, Vicki invites us to fully share in her adventure.

Canegarden Bay, Tortola

There are too many sailboats here.
To view just one, leaping in a turquoise sea with straining
    sails,
    would have been enough to dream on,
but so many, clustered together with masts empty to the sky,
    is a pity.

Waiting for the next week's sailors, many boats are empty
    now.
An empty hull, an empty song, an empty sea under a silent,
    cloudless sky.

We sailed into this photogenic bay in the early afternoon
    with steel-shouldered pelicans dive-bombing silver
    fingerlings hiding in tanned elk-horn coral.
Luckier sailboats were already tethered to the orange buoys,
    like bouncing basketballs on the growing waves.
On a sailboat you have to be fore-sighted, like the winners in
    chess:
Late arrivals anchor in the northern, outer limit of the bay,
    prey

to the sea-sickening pitch and rolls of the Atlantic Ocean
    wave-train.
Another sleepless night in paradise.
Should we have stayed at home and thought of here?

Steep sand crescent and gossiping palms matched the
    postcard I'd fingered for many years.
T-shirt shops set up on the beach with that temporary air of
    souvenir stands
    anywhere in the hurricane alley Caribbean.
The smoky restaurant was there, with a sandy buckled
    floor
    under a new tin roof set on slowly rotting wooden pillars.
We needed dinner reservations,
    not from any pretensions serving barefoot clientele,
    but from just-in-time inventory controls:
    the Island staff wouldn't buy fish or bread,
    and the grim, tired men wouldn't be there to play the
    short-lived
    tingling steel pan-Calypso music.
Oh, must we dream our dreams and have them too?

Another sleepless night:
    riding a three-pointed-sea on a rollercoaster bed
        pillow-first under anchor chains saber-rattling and
        straining
            to pull from the sand two stories (snorkeling depth)
            below
    anchor alarms sounding repeatedly
    grabbing for the boat-hook to ward off colliding boats
        until sleep clears to see the pitching tide set off false
        alarms
            moonlight waves crescendo, thundering on the hide-
            and-seek seawall.

But if we'd stayed at home, we couldn't imagine what we
    would have missed.
It would be a pity—not to have seen this plaid uniformed
    schoolgirl skipping
    in the late afternoon sun, shyly directing us to the only
    shop
    with bandaids on the six main islands, by taking our
    blistered hands,

—not to walk this dusty coast road to the rum distillery two
    centuries old,
    shaded by a grove of purple bananas, guarded by a dozing
        man and clouds of lacerating mosquitoes,

—not to breathe the yellow pollen of these thick-legged
    poinsettia trees,
    scarlet even in the sunset,

—not to be covered by an undulating layer of white butterflies
    so greedy for golden drips of nectar
    that even a waving hand
    repeatedly and delightedly
    can't displace them,

—not to know the homely joy of taking salt-free showers
    without a guard outside the door,
    without plugging in the quarters,
    without turning off the water that trickles while you soap,
    without shoes,

—not to finally understand the physics of a steep beach and
        the rib-cracking
    dangers in putting out to sea in a dingy from it,

—not to learn to trust your life to friends who have learned
    to trust you.

Vicki Brown Johnston

Your Turn

Most everyone who has ever traveled has probably asked Bishop's question: "Should we have stayed at home and thought of here?" Write a poem set in a "foreign" place, with the speaker reflecting on the wisdom of being in that place. Perhaps the protagonist has had to leave someone important at home to make the trip, or maybe events in the new place are not unfolding as she had planned. It does not matter whether or not you have traveled extensively: the foreign place may be the other side of the world, or it may just be the other side of town.

Your poem might answer any or all of the following questions of travel: Why are you there? How difficult was your journey? How do those you left behind feel about your going? How do your new surroundings compare with your old? What can you see, hear, taste, smell, and feel here that you can't find at home? When, if ever, will you return? How will you feel about going home?

Chapter Seventeen

Puzzle Poetry

In this chapter you will write a poem that takes the form of one or more mesostics. You have probably heard of or read about the more familiar **acrostic,** in which certain letters form a message when read in sequence. Typically, the initial letters of each line make a word when read downwards. When the words are the same across as they are down, the arrangement is called a **word square.** For instance:

GRAB

RARE

ARTS

BEST

While devices like these are amusing, they don't allow for much flexibility and can hardly be considered "poetic." A **mesostic,** on the other hand, in which *middle letters* of each line make another word when read downwards, offers a great deal of wiggle room. You can move the lines around to accommodate the middle letter you are using. The lines can be as long or as short as you choose.

It probably sounds more difficult to compose a mesostic than it actually is. The best way to explain it is simply to show an example. Here is John Cage's attempt. Although Cage uses the name "Mark Tobey" to form the many stanzas of his poem, we have, at best, an oblique portrait of the poet's friend. Instead, Cage gives us a wide-ranging semi-autobiography, full of the kind of observations we might expect to find in the author's diary.

25 Mesostics Re and Not Re Mark Tobey

it was iMpossible
 to do Anything:
the dooR
was locKed.

i won The first game.
 he wOn the second.
  in Boston,
   nExt
    Year, he'll be teaching philosophy.

the house is a Mess:
  pAintings
 wheRever
you looK.

she told Me
 his wAy
 of Reading
assumes that the booK he's reading is true.

why doesn'T
 he stOp painting?
  someBody
 will havE
 to spend Years cataloguing, etc.

The girl checking in the baggage
 reduced Our overweight to zero
  By counting it
 on a first-class passEnger's ticket: the heaviest handbag
had been hidden unnecessarilY

forTunately, we were with hanna,
 antOinette,
and hanna's two Boys.
 thE girl at the counter
gave one of the boYs a carry-on luggage tag as a souvenir.

My
 strAtegy:
act as though you'Re home;
 don't asK any questions.

instead of Music:
thunder, trAffic
        biRds, and high-speed military planes/producing sonic booms;
now and then a chicKen (pontpoint).

    each Thing he saw
he asked us tO look at.
        By
        thE time we reached the japanese restaurant
our eYes were open.

    the rooM
        dAvid has in the attic
        is veRy
good for his worK.

    how much do The paintings
        cOst?
    they were Bought
on the installmEnt plan:
there was no moneY.

    he played dominoes and drank calvados unTil
                fOur in the morning.
        carpenters came aBout
                sEven
            thirtY to finish their work in his bedroom.

    you can find ouT
        what kind Of art is up to the minute
        By visiting
        thE head office
of a successful advertising companY.

    i'M helpless
    i cAn't do a thing
    without Ritty in paris
and mimi in new yorK (artservices).

    "is There
anything yOu want
        Brought
    from thE
        citY?" no, nothing, less mass media, perhaps.

waiting for the bus, i happened to look at the paveMent
                i wAs standing on;
            noticed no diffeRence between
                looKing at art or away from it.

the chinese children accepted the freedoMs
            i gAve them
            afteR
        my bacK was turned.

pauline served lunch on The
        flOor
        But
        objEcted
    to the waY galka was using her knife and fork.

<pre>
            norTh
         Of paris, june '72:
         colly Bia platyphylla,
         plutEus cervinus, pholiota
mutabilis and several hYpholomas.

         The
      dOors and windows are open.
      "why Bring it back?
   i'd forgottEn where it was.
         You could have kept it."

         he told Me
            of A movie they'd seen,
         a natuRe film.
   he thought we would liKe it too.

         The paintings
   i had decided tO
            Buy
         wEre superfluous; nevertheless,
      after several Years, i owned them.

            sold Them
               tO write music, now there's a third.
      i must get the first two Back.
            whEre
            are theY?

   all it is is a Melody
      of mAny
      coloRs:
         Klangfarbenmelodie.
</pre>

                    John Cage

Many people, when asked to describe poetry, would depict it as a difficult, complicated essentially *serious* activity that has no room for fun. Yet even usually very pensive bards like John Keats, whom we tend to think of in connection with his odes to nightingales and melancholy and Grecian urns, are capable of writing lines like this:

> There was a naughty boy
> And a naughty boy was he,
> For nothing would he do
> But scribble poetry . . . .

Poetry, in short, can be a vehicle for pure play. Therefore, while there's nothing wrong with tackling important subjects, a poem does not have to uncover the meaning of life in order to bring pleasure to its readers.

John Cage, an innovator in music and art as well as writing, was a devotee of play. Probably his most famous "composition" is *4'33"*. In that piece, a pianist walks on stage and sits at a piano. However, instead of playing, he sits there for four minutes and thirty-three seconds. The ambient noise of the concert hall, the shuffling and murmuring of the audience members as they become increasingly uncomfortable, is the only "music."

Knowing that Cage was interested in experiments like that one, you may decide "25 Mesostics Re and Not Re Mark Tobey" is comparatively mainstream. Still, because this assignment may initially seem a bit tricky, two sample student poems are included. It is worth noting that neither of the student poets was particularly enamored of John Cage's poem. Both felt it went on too long, pushed the number of variations on Mark Tobey's name past the point of no return. (Cage, of course, would have argued that that was exactly what he meant to do.) Nevertheless, the students found the mesostic itself an inviting form. Using a vegetable as the "spine" of her poem, Jackie created a fresh, funny **ars poetica,** a summation of her ideas about how the art of poetry should be practiced. Kristi wrote a tender lyric about the nervousness a young man feels as he prepares to propose to his girlfriend.

how to
write
poetry

piCk
oUt
deliCious
jUicy
and Moist words that
dribBle down your chin
and pEpole
will savoR each wet crunch

Jackie Mitchell

★

Untitled

The Moon glistened
upon the midnight wAters.
They stRolled around the
boaRdwalk hand in hand,
nervouslY postponing the perfect moment.

The words Melting
on thE tip of his tongue.

Kristi Yurs

Your Turn

Whether or not you are particularly good at word games, chances are that at some time in your life you have sat down and worked a crossword puzzle or enjoyed a game of Scrabble or Boggle. This chapter encourages you to strengthen your skills in this area by asking you to write a poem composed of one or more mesostics.

The first thing you need to do when you compose a mesostic is to select the word or words that will form the poem's spine. Write the letters vertically, one letter per line, on your computer screen or a piece of paper. You should, like Cage and the student poets, do something to differentiate the key letters, whether you capitalize, italicize or put them in bold. Then look for ways to incorporate each letter into a line about the poem's subject. While you should organize your mesostic(s) around a central topic, give yourself ample opportunity to improvise and have fun. It is okay if the result is a little off-beat.

Suppose, to give a brief example, that I wanted to write a mesostic to my dog, Jake. First, I would write the letters of his name:

J
A
K
E

Then I would spend some time jotting down possible ways to use these letters. In a couple of minutes of scribbling, I come up with the lines, "you wag your tail and Jump / up to greet me eAch time / i turn my Key / in thE front door," which I align on the page to look like this:

you wag your tail and Jump
up to greet me eAch time
i turn my Key
in thE front door

Unacknowleged Kindnesses

Most of us will admit that there have been times when we did not acknowledge a kindness that we should have. Perhaps we felt shy about showing our appreciativeness, or maybe we simply forgot. Your poem for this chapter will give you an opportunity to make amends, to say thank you to someone to whom you are indebted.

Robert Hayden's debt is to his father. "Those Winter Sundays" is his belated note of thanks. Yet for all its heartfelt emotion, this is a spooky poem. The speaker, presumably an adult, is thinking back on the early mornings when his father would build a fire before the rest of the family awoke. The father also polishes his son's shoes for church. He is apparently a thoughtful man. Nevertheless, the poem is full of words and phrases suggesting violence. The cold is "blueblack" like a bruise; the speaker's hands are "cracked"; he can hear "the cold splintering, breaking"; and he fears "the chronic angers of that house." The small comforts provided evidently come with a price.

Still, the son has finally come to realize that what he owes his father is important, that the time has come for him to recognize the love he received. The answer to the final question, "What did I know, what did I know / of love's austere and lonely offices?" is *Almost nothing.*

Those Winter Sundays

Sundays too my father got up early
and put his clothes on in the blueblack cold,
then with cracked hands that ached
from labor in the weekday weather made
banked fires blaze. No one ever thanked him.

I'd wake and hear the cold splintering, breaking.
When the rooms were warm, he'd call,
and slowly I would rise and dress,
fearing the chronic angers of that house,

Speaking indifferently to him,
who had driven out the cold
and polished my good shoes as well.
What did I know, what did I know
of love's austere and lonely offices?

Robert Hayden

It is not necessary to learn something about a writer's life to appreciate a good poem, but a little information about Robert Hayden's situation does deepen "Those Winter Sundays." Hayden was a foster child who grew up in an impoverished working-class family. He was raised by foster parents, although he kept in touch with his birth parents. He felt indebted to the "folk" who raised him, yet, not surprisingly, throughout his childhood he longed to escape his surroundings, the Detroit slum known as Paradise Valley. Hayden's poem is suffused with this tension between gratitude and apprehensiveness.

Kelly's poem "Just for Me" is also autobiographical and also focuses on a family situation, although the mood is decidedly less troubled. The poem describes a private "ritual of Thanksgiving." The speaker, after greeting her grandmother in the kitchen, is given a clandestine piece of pie before the actual meal begins. While this transgression is certainly a mild one (presumably the worst punishment the granddaughter and grandmother can receive is a scolding from the child's mother) the slight conspiracy seems to bring them closer together. Much of the poem's poignancy is implied. "Just for Me" is directly addressed to the older woman, but it leaves open the possibility that she has passed away, that it may now be too late for the granddaughter to fully acknowledge her grandmother's kindness.

Just for Me

I can still feel
the worn-out softness
of your jade cotton pullover
against my cheek as you
greet me with a gentle embrace.

I can still smell
White Linen perfume
carefully dabbed on your wrists,
the turkey basting in the oven
as you clasp my cheeks to kiss me.

I can still see
the cluttered kitchen and the
homemade pumpkin pie just for me
on top of your black-and-white television
as you search through the silverware drawer.

I can still hear
you whisper, "Don't tell your mother":
the ritual of Thanksgiving—dessert
before the feast. You glide
the knife through my pie.

I can still taste
the divine combination of Cool Whip,
chilled pumpkin, and flaky crust
as only you could make it;
I hide behind your protective frame
indulging in that first piece of pie.

Kelly Janssen

Your Turn

All of us at some time or another have benefited from yet failed to acknowledge the generosity of others. Write a poem in which you recall an instance of kindness for which you were either too busy, too rude, or, like the speaker in Robert Hayden's poem, too ignorant to show your gratitude.

If you have trouble getting started, consider the following **prewriting** (or early writing) strategies. Sometimes drawing on ideas that are as old as Aristotle, scholars in rhetoric and composition have defined, described, and categorized a number of methods writers can use in the invention stage of composing. Probably the most widely known and commonly employed of these strategies is **freewriting.** When you freewrite, you park yourself in front of your computer screen or take out pen and paper and write, nonstop, for a short, predetermined period of time. Some people write for as few as five minutes, others prefer to keep going for up to twenty. The important thing is that you write the *entire* time. If you cannot think of anything to say, you write, "I cannot think of anything to say," until you *can* think of something. Do not worry about grammar, punctuation, or spelling. No one is going to see this but you. When you are finished, go back through your freewrite and, like a miner panning for gold, look for whatever is worth saving. If you do not always find a nugget, there are usually at least a few shiny, valuable flakes.

Another method of prewriting commonly employed in composition classes, which can be used with equal effectiveness when writing poetry, is **clustering** or **brainstorming.** Like freewriting, clustering encourages you to turn off your inner censor and turn on your imagination. However, whereas freewriting is fairly chaotic, clustering imposes some order on what you come up with. As you jot down words or phrases that come into your head, you may notice patterns beginning to emerge. If ideas and images seem to be related, you cluster them together. And if clusters of images seem connected, you draw lines between those clusters.

If you are lucky or inspired, there may not be any need to prewrite. You can get to the main event right away. There will be times, though, when getting started is difficult. Under those circumstances, it is nice to have a couple of prewriting techniques that you can draw on.

Chapter Nineteen

Rendezvous Unkept

Everyone has had the infuriating experience of waiting for someone or something that does not show up. Your poem for this chapter gives you a chance to write about this rendezvous unkept. Whether it is a blind date who blew you off, or a bus that never came, or some wholly imaginary incident, as in the poem below by Muriel Rukeyser, the subject of your poem will allow you to create or re-create a time when things did not go as you had planned.

"Waiting for Icarus" updates a very old myth. In the Greek original, Icarus and his father, Daedalus, have been imprisoned on the island of Crete. An inventor, Daedalus has devised a means of escape. He makes wings of feathers and wax, and he and Icarus put them on and fly away. Daedalus has cautioned Icarus not to go too high, but once they are aloft, Icarus is so carried away by the joy of flight that he soars up toward the sun until it melts his wax, his feathers fall out, and he plummets to the sea. Over the centuries, the subject has proved to be a fascinating one for writers and artists. (In fact, two of the other poets in this book, W. H. Auden and William Carlos Williams, have written well-known poems about Icarus.) What is especially intriguing about the myth is that it points out humanity's insatiable yearning to explore and create, while also demonstrating the consequences of unchecked curiosity.

For Muriel Rukeyser, however, Icarus is less interesting than the woman he left behind. Creating a new unnamed character, Rukeyser gives us an entirely novel take on the situation. Rather than an intrepid hero, Icarus comes across as a heel ("He said he would be back and we'd drink wine together / He said that everything would be better than before") and something of a coward ("He said he would never again cringe before his father"). On the other hand, while his girlfriend may have been a bit of a dupe, ultimately she sounds more adventurous than her boyfriend: "I would have liked to try those wings myself. / It would have been better than this."

Perhaps the most striking formal feature of "Waiting for Icarus" is its use of anaphora. Simply put, **anaphora** is the repetition of initial words or phrases in successive clauses, sentences, or stanzas. It is a common rhetorical device you have seen many times, although you probably did not know what to call it. In this poem, the examples of anaphora are "He said" and "I remember." Used skillfully, as it is here, anaphora creates a powerful rhythm that helps to drive a writer's point home.

Waiting for Icarus

He said he would be back and we'd drink wine together
He said that everything would be better than before
He said we were on the edge of a new relation
He said he would never again cringe before his father
He said that he was going to invent full-time
He said he loved me that going into me
He said he was going into the world and the sky
He said all the buckles were very firm
He said the wax was the best wax
He said Wait for me here on the beach
He said Just don't cry

I remember the gulls and the waves
I remember the islands going dark on the sea
I remember the girls laughing
I remember they said he only wanted to get away from me
I remember mother saying: Inventors are like poets, a trashy
    lot
I remember she told me those who try out inventions are
    worse
I remember she added: Women who love such are the worst
    of all

I have been waiting all day, or perhaps longer.
I would have liked to try those wings myself.
It would have been better than this.

Muriel Rukeyser

A **dramatic monologue** is a poem in which the speaker takes on the identity of some person other than himself or herself, like Rukeyser becoming Icarus's girlfriend. The speaker addresses a specific listener or listeners whose replies—if there are any—we cannot hear. Typically, in the course of a dramatic monologue the person unintentionally reveals a great many things about his or her disposition, desires, fears, and flaws. Because the poem is "spoken" in character, the poet must work to carefully capture the distinctiveness and eccentricities of the individual's speech. (A related form of address is the **soliloquy,** in which a person talks to himself or herself as though thinking aloud yet unable to be heard by an audience.)

Among the many poets who have shown a special gift for writing in the form are Robert Browning and Alfred Tennyson in England, and T. S. Eliot, Robert Frost, and Muriel Rukeyser in the United States. In "Waiting for Icarus," the dramatic monologue allows the latter poet to explore male-female relationships from an unexpected perspective and from a distinctly feminist slant.

Katy Montgomery's "Last Letter" focuses on the present instead of the long-ago past. In further contrast to the model poem, Katy's response is based on her own life experience. "Last Letter" traces the gradually disintegrating relationship between two childhood friends. While the speaker continues living in one place, her friend "migrated east / and west." They keep in touch through the mail, drawing pictures of "daisies, suns, and sailboats" on their letters, talking about favorite movies, discussing family secrets. Over time, though, the "magic missiles" grow "sparser every year," until, finally, the speaker realizes that it has been a year since she has heard from her friend. Sadly, she leaves us wondering if they will ever communicate again.

Last Letter

They migrated east
and west for years.
Stickered envelopes
with our addresses
first in scrawling scribbles,
and then in the handwriting
we knew each other by.

Artists, we garnished
the pages with our
daisies, suns, and sailboats.
Critics, we commended our

favorite movies and songs.
Informants, we divulged
our families' secrets.

Magic missiles transported
our aspirations, our heartbreaks,
our souls a thousand miles.
Growing sparser every year,
their allurement fading,
you received my last
letter a year ago, but
my mailbox still stands

empty.

Katy Montgomery

Your Turn

Write a poem in which you or an imaginary character are waiting for someone or something that never arrives. You might want to answer the following questions in your poem: Who is the speaker? What is her personality like? Is she confident and cocky, or nervous and fearful? What is her relationship to the thing or person for whom she is waiting? Why is she waiting now rather than later? How long has she been waiting? Does she believe her waiting is in vain? What will happen if the thing or person doesn't show up?

Chapter Twenty

Undermining the Poem

Creative writing students are often warned by their teachers, with good reason, that the easiest way to ruin a poem or story is by denying, at the end, that any of the events ever took place. The classic example of this gambit occurs when the narrator, often in the person of the writer herself, wakes up one morning to discover that she has had a run of unprecedented good fortune. Perhaps she learns that she has won the lottery, been elected president, and been awarded a Nobel Peace Prize, all in the span of twenty-four hours. Naturally, readers know this cannot happen in real life, but they also know that the rules are different in the world of poetry and fiction. It is okay to exaggerate, to get carried away. So it comes as disappointment when the writer, seemingly guilt-stricken by her dishonesty, suddenly realizes the preposterousness of the situation and announces: "And then the alarm went off. Everything that happened was just a dream!"

The assignment for this chapter, however, asks you to come dangerously close to that taboo ending. What you will be doing is creating a miniature world in the body of your poem, then undercutting it at the very end. The difference between the "alarm clock poem" and this one is that you are deliberately leading your reader toward a revelation of your deception. The disillusionment he feels is the point of the poem, not an unintended aftereffect.

In Weldon Kees's poem "For My Daughter," the speaker is watching his daughter not long after she has awakened in the morning. However, instead of the thoughts we would expect a parent to have—happiness at being with his child, hope for her future—he sees "Concealed, hintings of death she does not heed." The poem goes on to speculate about a number of awful fates that might befall the girl: she may freeze to death or drown; she will grow old and ugly; she may die in a war or marry an unworthy man. Then, suddenly, Kees states: "I have no daughter. I desire none," and we are relieved to find out the speaker is not a father. (Someone as unrelentingly gloomy as he is should probably avoid parenthood altogether!)

For My Daughter

Looking into my daughter's eyes I read
Beneath the innocence of morning flesh
Concealed, hintings of death she does not heed.
Coldest of winds have blown this hair, and mesh
Of seaweed snarled these miniatures of hands;
The night's slow poison, tolerant and bland,
Has moved her blood. Parched years that I have seen
That may be hers appear: foul, lingering
Death in certain war, the slim legs green.
Or, fed on hate, she relishes the sting
Of others' agony; perhaps the cruel
Bride of a syphilitic or a fool.
These speculations sour in the sun.
I have no daughter. I desire none.

Weldon Kees

"For My Daughter" is a **sonnet,** which is a fourteen-line poem written in iambic pentameter (five beats per line). In the **Italian,** or **Petrarchan, sonnet** (which was supposedly perfected by the 14th-century Italian poet Petrarch), there is an eight-line **octave** followed by a six-line **sestet.** Traditionally, the octave develops an idea that the sestet completes. The turning point between the two parts is called the *volta.* The Petrarchan rhyme scheme is an *abbaabba* octave with a *cdecde* sestet, or some variation on those three rhymes.

In an **English,** or **Shakespearean, sonnet,** there are three quatrains, which rhyme *abab cdcd efef,* followed by a couplet rhyming *gg.* In a true Shakespearean sonnet, each quatrain deals with a distinct part of the theme. The couplet sums up all that has gone before. (For a student version of a Shakespearean sonnet, see Frank Avery's experiment in Chapter Forty-Seven.)

Like other American poets before and after him, Kees takes some liberties with the form. (Many of Robert Lowell's later "sonnets," for instance, do not rhyme at all.) Kees uses an unconventional rhyme scheme: *ababccdedeffgg*. There is no octave or sestet. And the turning point does not come until the very end, in the thirteenth line. Nevertheless, despite all its deviations, "For My Daughter" is recognizably a sonnet.

As in nearly every chapter of *Poetry Writing*, the response poem you write asks you to look at the content of the model poem rather than its form. However, if you decide that you would like to challenge yourself and write a sonnet, you will probably want to read more examples to get a better feel for what is required. The most famous sonnets in English are by Shakespeare and are usually included in collections of his plays. Most libraries will also have copies of books by the following poets who have written extensively (and fairly accessibly) in the form: William Wordsworth, Dante Gabriel Rossetti, Elizabeth Barrett Browning, E. A. Robinson, and Edna St. Vincent Millay.

Beth Sheehan found that the sonnet form did not help her towards the poem she wanted to write, so "Burn" is in free verse. A person who is often around cigarette smokers, Beth has carefully observed their behavior, watched their faces as they breathe the "deep / dusty fog" into their lungs and "expel a haze / that makes reality fade." Throughout the poem, she sounds convincingly like a confirmed smoker, someone who is always craving one more cancer stick. Yet the final two lines reveal "I don't smoke / and never will." Like Kees, Beth leaves her readers feeling glad that the situation she has described is a fantasy.

Burn

I want to light a match
and watch the day dance
into the distance of the past
and burn hard memories with the flame
that lights my cigarette.

The ashes will fall
clumsily to the ground
like the disarray
of mindless notions
scattered through my brain.

And the cigarette
will slowly shrink
into nothing—
and the nothing
will soon reside in me.

As I breathe a deep
dusty fog into my lungs,
I'll expel a haze
that makes reality fade
from my eyes.

I want to smoke
three packs a day,
and let each drag
burn my strain.

But I don't smoke
and never will.

Beth Sheehan

Your Turn

Write a poem in which you, like Weldon Kees and Beth Sheehan, create a fully imagined world. In the last line or lines, let the reader know that everything that has come before was a lie.

Both Kees and Beth construct worlds that are increasingly unpleasant. In the end, when they pull back the curtain to reveal the truth, we are happy to return to situations that are less desolate than we had feared. Of course, you may choose the opposite approach. If so, your poem would move toward a sunny picture of life, only to have it ultimately disappear.

If you decide to venture into the sonnet for this assignment, you will probably best be served by the Shakespearean form. This will allow you to build up your fantasy quatrain by quatrain. Then, in the concluding couplet, you can sabotage the previous twelve lines.

Chapter Twenty-One

Un-Memorials

Your poem for this chapter will commemorate an event that did *not* occur. This will require you to do some negative thinking: What near-incident are you most glad never happened? Or, conversely, what do you wish had taken place that never did?

For William Stafford, a conscientious objector during World War II, one of the nonevents most worth celebrating is a war that was not fought, in this case between the United States and Canada. The poem is set at an actual memorial, the International Peace Garden in North Dakota, but Stafford wisely chooses not to name the location. Instead, he gives the place an air of mystery: "This is the field where grass joined hands," he writes; "Birds fly here without any sound." Fittingly for a poem about the absence of human conflict, there are no people present in the poem.

The world is full of monuments: monuments to presidents and great generals and sports stars, monuments heralding inventions and the founding of cities, and monuments to battles.

Stafford's monument, however, is a poem. Much of his voluminous work is in free verse, but here his stanzas rhyme *abccb dadee,* which gives "At the Un-National Monument" the succinctness of an epitaph. One feels as though the poem is suitable for inscription on an obelisk or shrine, although Stafford would probably prefer that it remain on paper—or simply be written on the wind.

At the Un-National Monument Along the Canadian Border

This is the field where the battle did not happen,
where the unknown soldier did not die.
This is the field where grass joined hands,
where no monument stands,
and the only heroic thing is the sky.

Birds fly here without any sound,
unfolding their wings across the open.
No people killed—or were killed—on this ground
hallowed by neglect and an air so tame
that people celebrate it by forgetting its name.

William Stafford

Both Stafford and Matt Heintzelman venerate "ground / hallowed by neglect," although Matt's poem records a nonevent of more narrowly personal significance. In "The Place," a man revisits his old high school with his son. Evidently the boy relishes tales of athletic exploits, for his father begins to talk about football, swimming, and baseball. Yet in each new stanza we learn of the things the father *did not* accomplish: he *did not* run for three touchdowns, he *did not* win the 100-meter breaststroke, he *did not* pitch the game-winning strikeout. What, the son wants to know, *did* his father do in high school? When his father tells him that he received straight A's, the boy responds with a disappointed "Oh." This anticlimactic ending is in sharp contrast to the ringing pacifism of Stafford's concluding couplet. Nevertheless, both poems suggest that it is not always the most visible accomplishment that is the most important: the endings of both poems are ironic.

"Irony" is a term we use often, without always knowing exactly what it means. In part, that may be because, from a rhetorician's standpoint, there are so many types of it. (See Wayne Booth's classic, *A Rhetoric of Irony,* if you are especially interested in this topic.) For our purposes, the three most common types of irony found in poetry are verbal, situational, and dramatic.

Verbal irony occurs when people use words to convey the opposite of what they mean. You would spot this sort of irony immediately if someone were to tell you, "Have a nice day," just before he put a pistol to your head and pulled the trigger.

Dramatic irony occurs when characters in a work of literature are unaware of what the audience knows. If, for instance, Stafford had introduced a character—a patriotic veteran, say—who wandered around the un-national monument while believing he was at a war memorial, the situation would make for dramatic irony.

And Matt's "The Place" makes use of **situational irony.** There is an incongruity between what we expect to happen when a father takes his son to his old school (he will brag about all the things he had done there) and the reality of what actually happens (he talks about all the things he did not do).

The Place

Here we are, son.
This is the spot where
you can see it all.

See what?

Right over there, on the
grass, is where I didn't run
for three touchdowns in
the state championships.

And over there, inside
that fieldhouse, is where
I didn't win the 100 meter
breaststroke against Central.

To your right, over there on
that diamond is where I didn't
strike out Bobby Douglas in the
bottom of the ninth to send us
to sectionals.

And on those courts over there . . .

Dad . . . did you do anything?

I got straight A's.

Oh.

M. Vincent Heintzelman

Your Turn

Write a poem that memorializes an event that did *not* occur. The poem may, like Stafford's, reflect on a public occasion, such as a war. Or, like Matt, you may decide to write about something more personal—the time you did not talk back to your father, for example, or the vacation you were going to take to Florida that would have landed you in the center of a hurricane.

It may help your poem if you address some or all of these questions: Why is the nonevent important? What, specifically, would have happened? Whom would it have affected? Why did it not take place? How has its nonoccurrence changed your life?

Chapter Twenty-Two

Fantasy Meets Reality

The life people live in their heads often contrasts sharply with the one that takes place elsewhere. Sometimes the interior life allows us relief from the harshness of an outer truth. At other times, this inwardness can have dire consequences. Chapter Twenty-two asks you to consider either possibility and write a poem in which someone's imaginary existence clashes with real life.

In the poem below, one of her most famous, Gwendolyn Brooks plunges into the mind of the wife of the man who murdered Emmett Till. While the poem is fairly self-explanatory, it may help to have a little historical background. Emmett Till was a fourteen-year-old African American from Chicago who was visiting relatives in Mississippi in the summer of 1955. Friends described him as playful and outgoing. He seems, also, to have been somewhat unaware of the marked difference between life in the North and South. After he "wolf-whistled" at Carolyn Bryant, the protagonist of the poem, the woman's husband, Roy, and a friend named J. W. Milam decided to defend her honor. Although the evidence over-whelmingly suggested that the defendants should be convicted or murder, they were acquitted by an all-white jury. The trial was covered by the national media, and many African Americans—Martin Luther King Jr. among them—were inspired by this injus-tice to continue their pursuit of a vigorous campaign for civil rights.

The poem's central conflict revolves around the dissonance between the woman's initial fantasy of her husband as a "Fine Prince" and her eventual realization that he is, in fact, a "Dark Villain." Brooks does a superb job of interweaving the woman's thoughts with the mundane chores of cooking dinner and feeding her family. By the end of the poem, when her prince's mouth, "wet and red, / So very, very, very red," closes over her own, we are unexpectedly sympathetic to the protagonist. She seems finally to realize that if young, harmless Emmett Till is not safe from violence, neither are her own children. (An interesting postscript: shortly after the trial concluded, Car-olyn Bryant divorced her husband.)

A Bronzeville Mother Loiters in Mississippi. Meanwhile, a Mississippi Mother Burns Bacon

From the first it had been like a
Ballad. It had the beat inevitable. It had the blood.
A wildness cut up, and tied in little bunches,
Like the four-line stanzas of the ballads she had never quite
Understood—the ballads they had set her to, in school.

Herself: the milk-white maid, the "maid mild"
Of the ballad. Pursued
By the Dark Villain. Rescued by the Fine Prince.
The Happiness-Ever-After.
That was worth anything.
It was good to be a "maid mild."
That made the breath go fast.

Her bacon burned. She
Hastened to hide it in the step-on can, and
Drew more strips from the meat case. The eggs and sour-
      milk biscuits
Did well. She set out a jar
Of her new quince preserve.

. . . But there was a something about the matter of the Dark
      Villain.
He should have been older, perhaps.
The hacking down of a villain was more fun to think about
When his menace possessed undisputed breadth, undisputed
      height,
And a harsh kind of vice.

And best of all, when his history was cluttered
With the bones of many eaten knights and princesses.

The fun was disturbed, then all but nullified
When the Dark Villain was a blackish child
Of fourteen, with eyes still too young to be dirty,
And a mouth too young to have lost every reminder
Of its infant softness.

That boy must have been surprised! For
These were grown-ups. Grown-ups were supposed to be
    wise.
And the Fine Prince—and that other—so tall, so broad, so
Grown! Perhaps the boy had never guessed
That the trouble with grown-ups was that under the
    magnificent shell of adulthood, just under,
Waited the baby full of tantrums.
It occurred to her that there may have been something
Ridiculous in the picture of the Fine Prince
Rushing (rich with the breadth and height and
Mature solidness whose lack, in the Dark Villain, was
    impressing her,
Confronting her more and more as this first day after the
    trial
And acquittal wore on) rushing
With his heavy companion to hack down (unhorsed)
That little foe.
So much had happened, she could not remember now what
    that foe had done
Against her, or if anything had been done.
The one thing in the world that she did know and knew
With terrifying clarity was that her composition
Had disintegrated. That, although the pattern prevailed,
The breaks were everywhere. That she could think
Of no thread capable of the necessary
Sew-work.

She made the babies sit in their places at the table.
Then, before calling Him, she hurried
To the mirror with her comb and lipstick. It was necessary
To be more beautiful than ever.
The beautiful wife.
For sometimes she fancied he looked at her as though
Measuring her. As if he considered, Had she been worth It?

Had *she* been worth the blood, the cramped cries, the little
    stuttering bravado,
The gradual dulling of those Negro eyes,
The sudden, overwhelming *little-boyness* in that barn?
Whatever she might feel or half-feel, the lipstick necessity
    was something apart. He must never conclude
That she had not been worth It.

He sat down, the Fine Prince, and
Began buttering a biscuit. He looked at his hands.
He twisted in his chair, he scratched his nose.
He glanced again, almost secretly, at his hands.
More papers were in from the North, he mumbled. More
    meddling headlines.
With their pepper-words, "bestiality," and "barbarism," and
"Shocking."
The half-sneers he had mastered for the trial worked across
His sweet and pretty face.

What he'd like to do, he explained, was kill them all.
The time lost. The unwanted fame.
Still, it had been fun to show those intruders
A thing or two. To show that snappy-eyed mother,
That sassy, Northern, brown-black—

Nothing could stop Mississippi.
He knew that. Big Fella
Knew that.
And, what was so good, Mississippi knew that.
Nothing and nothing could stop Mississippi.
They could send in their petitions, and scar
Their newspapers with bleeding headlines. Their governors
Could appeal to Washington . . .

"What I want," the older baby said, "is 'lasses on my jam."
Whereupon the younger baby
Picked up the molasses pitcher and threw
The molasses in his brother's face. Instantly
The Fine Prince leaned across the table and slapped
The small and smiling criminal.
She did not speak. When the Hand
Came down and away, and she could look at her child,
At her baby-child,

She could think only of blood.
Surely her baby's cheek
Had disappeared, and in its place, surely,
Hung a heaviness, a lengthening red, a red that had no end.
She shook her head. It was not true, of course.
It was not true at all. The
Child's face was as always, the
Color of the paste in her paste-jar.

She left the table, to the tune of the children's lamentations,
    which were shriller
Than ever. She
Looked out of a window. She said not a word. *That*
Was one of the new Somethings—
The fear,
Tying her as with iron.

Suddenly she felt his hands upon her. He had followed her
To the window. The children were whimpering now.
Such bits of tots. And she, their mother,
Could not protect them. She looked at her shoulders, still
Gripped in the claim of his hands. She tried, but could not
    resist the idea
That a red ooze was seeping, spreading darkly, thickly,
    slowly,
Over her white shoulders, her own shoulders,
And over all of Earth and Mars.

He whispered something to her, did the Fine Prince,
    something
About love, something about love and night and intention.
She heard no hoof-beat of the horse and saw no flash of the
    shining steel.

He pulled her face around to meet
His, and there it was, close, close,
For the first time in all those days and nights.
His mouth, wet and red,
So very, very, very red,
Closed over hers.

Then a sickness heaved within her. The courtroom Coca-Cola,
The courtroom beer and hate and sweat and drone,

Pushed like a wall against her. She wanted to bear it.
But his mouth would not go away and neither would the
Decapitated exclamation points in that Other Woman's eyes.

She did not scream.
She stood there.
But a hatred for him burst into glorious flower,
And its perfume enclasped them—big,
Bigger than all magnolias.

The last bleak news of the ballad.
The rest of the rugged music.
The last quatrain.

Gwendolyn Brooks

Sometimes the line between a long poem like this one and a short story can be thin. "A Bronzeville Mother" is a **narrative poem**—a poem that tells a story. If we start with *Beowulf*, narrative poetry is as old as poetry written in English. In twentieth-century America alone, there have been far more outstanding narrative poems than we have room to list. In this book alone, we could, to name a few, include T. S. Eliot's "The Journey of the Magi," Anne Sexton's "Cinderella" and Gary Soto's "Mexicans Begin Jogging."

But how do you tell the difference between a poem and a short story? The simplest way is to look at the right margin of the page. If it is ragged, that means the writer has consciously decided to break the lines so that they end on an emphatic word, or pause in such a way that the reader is curious to know what will come next. Some of Brooks's lines are very long, others consist of only a word or two. In every case, though, she takes maximum advantage of the flexibility that poetry offers to orchestrate a reader's responses to the narrative. She can come down hard and fast to emphasize "Shocking" in the eighth stanza, then, five stanzas later, linger on a line with an altogether different sound and feeling, the sluggish yet terrifying "a red ooze was seeping, spreading darkly, thickly, slowly."

"A Bronzeville Mother" is the longest poem in this book; however, as Maggie Pielsticker's "Princess of Virgins" shows, your own poem need not be nearly as long. In Maggie's poem, the clash between reality and fantasy is embodied in the unnamed protagonist. On the outside, the Princess of Virgins is "Sitcom perfect," but this facade merely camouflages the troubled girl underneath. We suspect there may be something wrong in the middle of the poem when we learn she "wore her sleeves long / to cover up ugly secrets," and we find by the end that our suspicions were well founded as the poet leaves us with the grotesque image of "virgin white skin / painted in blood."

Princess of Virgins

Her friends gave her the nickname
after watching some sitcom
where the girl was perfect.
Sitcom perfect.
Just like her.
Princess of Virgins
who wore her hair long
in flowing curls down her back
because it looked pretty.
Princess of Virgins
who wore her sleeves long
to cover up ugly secrets
because they didn't look pretty.
The sitcom-perfect Princess of Virgins
sat alone in her room.
No sex.
No drugs.
Just a knife
and virgin white skin
painted in blood.

Maggie Pielsticker

Your Turn

Write a poem in which a fantasy world comes in conflict with the realities of daily life. "A Bronzeville Mother" and "Princess of Virgins" tell the story of two such confrontations. They are grim and unforgiving pieces. Your poem, of course, does not have to be. You may well decide to write about someone who remains unflinchingly optimistic in the face of affliction.

Even if your character does not have a firm grasp of the difference between truth and fantasy, you as the author should. Once again, you may find it easier to respond to the prompt if you are guided by a focused set of questions: Does your character realize he or she is out of touch with ordinary life? Is the person a hero or a heel in his or her imaginative life? Does anyone else figure prominently in the character's fantasy? If so, what is that person's real relationship to the character? Why has the character created a vivid alternative imaginative life in the first place? What problems in the character's real life can be ameliorated only by fantasy? When do fantasy and reality clash most? When do they leave each other alone? Is the resulting situation primarily comic, tragic, or a little of both?

Chapter Twenty-Three

Too Far Down

Everyone has felt depressed at times. We all know how it is, to paraphrase the old blues lyric, to be so far down that we might not be able to get back up again. Your poem for this chapter should recount a period in your life when you felt "too far down" to continue much further.

The poet providing the theme for your variation is Robert Lowell, a man both brilliant and deeply troubled. Although he wrote some of the most dazzling American poems of the middle twentieth century, Lowell suffered from often debilitating depression throughout his adult life. Periods of depression would usually be preceded by a mania in which he talked and wrote furiously. These facts might be irrelevant in another poet's biography, but for Lowell his own mental health served as the subject matter of some of his finest poems.

Still, "Skunk Hour" suggests more than it states the severity of Lowell's depression. Granted, he acknowledges, "My mind's not right," and he says, "I hear / my ill-spirit sob in each blood cell, / as if my hand were at its throat . . . ." Yet most of the poem concentrates on the landscape around the poet and the people who inhabit it. He remarks on the rich old woman who seems to run Nautilus Island and the summer millionaire who has apparently fallen on hard times (his yacht has been auctioned off to lobstermen). These apparently unrelated incidents lead him to conclude that "The season's ill."

The poem's climax comes when the speaker surprises a family of skunks who are devouring his garbage late at night. Rather than viewing them as mere nuisances, he sees the skunks as sinister. Their "moonstruck eyes' red fire" contrasts with the "chalk-dry and spar spire / of the Trinitarian Church" and they "will not scare." The skunks are the final and most powerful emblem of the speaker's own fears.

Skunk Hour
(for Elizabeth Bishop)

Nautilus Island's hermit
heiress still lives through winter in her Spartan cottage;
her sheep still graze above the sea.
Her son's a bishop. Her farmer
is first selectman in our village;
she's in her dotage.

Thirsting for
the hierarchic privacy
of Queen Victoria's century,
she buys up all
the eyesores facing her shore,
and lets them fall.

The season's ill—
we've lost our summer millionaire,
who seemed to leap from an L. L. Bean
catalogue. His nine-knot yawl
was auctioned off to lobstermen.
A red fox stain covers Blue Hill.

And now our fairy
decorator brightens his shop for fall;
his fishnet's filled with orange cork,
orange, his cobbler's bench and awl;
there is no money in his work,
he'd rather marry.

One dark night,
my Tudor Ford climbed the hill's skull;
I watched for love-cars. Lights turned down,
they lay together, hull to hull,

where the graveyard shelves on the town . . . .
My mind's not right.

A car radio bleats,
"Love, O careless Love . . . ." I hear
my ill-spirit sob in each blood cell,
as if my hand were at its throat . . . .
I myself am hell;
nobody's here—

only skunks, that search
in the moonlight for a bite to eat.
They march on their soles up Main Street:
white stripes, moonstruck eyes' red fire
under the chalk-dry and spar spire
of the Trinitarian Church.

I stand on top
of our back steps and breathe the rich air—
a mother skunk with her column of kittens swills the
garbage pail.
She jabs her wedge-head in a cup
of sour cream, drops her ostrich tail,
and will not scare.

Robert Lowell

Robert Lowell's *Life Studies* (1959), from which "Skunk Hour" is taken, is generally thought to be a milestone in **confessional poetry.** If you have never heard this term before, it may strike you as redundant. After all, as a number of critics have pointed out, it is often difficult for first-person lyric poetry *not* to be confessional. However, in the 1950s and 1960s, some very important poets began discussing their moral, emotional, and physical life in frank and intimate terms. Aside from Lowell, other poets in this book who are typically considered "confessional" include Sylvia Plath, Anne Sexton, James Wright, and perhaps Allen Ginsberg. (Elizabeth Bishop, to whom Lowell addresses his poem, also suffered from depression, but she was far more guarded in disclosing the details of her personal life.)

By the early 1970s, confessional poetry had become the norm, and the directness with which poets revealed embarrassing details about themselves was no longer as shocking. The cumulative effect of all this explicit revelation—combined with the suicides of Sylvia Plath in 1963, John Berryman in 1972, and Anne Sexton in 1974—made many people renounce confessional poetry as a one-way road leading inevitably to nihilism. These critics called for a return to poetry that was less self-centered and more concerned with the social and political issues of the larger world.

Whether or not that call was ever seriously heeded is open to debate. Critics of mainstream poetry complain that too many poets, especially those who teach in colleges and universities, write with very little authority about any subject other than themselves. Be that as it may, it is difficult to deny that nearly all poets will, at least occasionally, want to find a place for the autobiographical in their poetry. Many of us (rightfully, I think) feel that our own lives contain vital poetic material that we ignore at our own risk.

Sarah Brown's "Gray" may or may not be about her own life—in this instance that probably does not much matter. We do know that "Gray" is spoken in the first-person from the point of view of a long-distance runner as she makes her way steadily through a familiar but nevertheless depressing landscape. Like Lowell, Sarah lets objects the speaker sees carry much of the emotional weight of the poem. From the gray waves on the lake and the dead frog and fish on the road to the fallen hedge apples that have been run over by cars and grotesquely remind the speaker of smashed brains, everything she observes contributes to a feeling of despair and world-weariness. This dejection is emphasized by the refrains that appear in the second half of the poem: "I will not die soon" and "Can I please be done yet? / Please?"

Gray

The waves on the lake
are choppy and gray
like the sky slightly lighter.

A frog old and smushed
is a leathery patch
on the road and a fish
just a few days dead
lies ahead, still retaining
three gutted dimensions.

If there was sun,
this would be a scene
for a nature calendar,
but now even the cedar
A-frame on the point
seems dull. Full, robust
leaves hang limply on
the trees and the single
birdsong sounds tired.

Rain is not predicted.

The fat old woman who
lives in the court is
the only other person about,
her trained-to-maim
Doberman pinscher
pulls at the leash.
She won't be able
to hold it for long.
Like the last one, it
will soon discover
the canine pleasure
of teeth sinking in flaccid
human flesh.
Or maybe this new carnivore
prefers younger, firmer meat.

My step does not hasten.

There are no window lights.
No driveway cars. Not even
a sprinkler in the spiteful heat.
The air looks cold but I sweat
in shorts and a sallow yellow shirt.

Can I please be done yet?
Please?

Two more miles wind ahead
on this blackish tar bubble road.
Two more miles to prove I am athletic,
not a tubby couch-warmer-
American the magazines say
will die soon.

I will not die soon.

My heart thumps fast
in a regular rhythm.
My breath is harsh
but sure. My legs are
automatic spaghetti and
there is no hint of a burn.
Two miles or more, I will
not die soon.

A squirrel scurries
in the road ahead.
Undecided. Left? Right?
The white car approaching
is not slowing,
its windows are dark.
The undecided squirrel catches
on black rubber, tumbles beneath
speeding wheels, black rubber, black
tar mesh with gold fur
and bloody innards.

I do not wince, or alter rhythm.
My breath is harsh but sure.

Hedge apples cover the road
from a tall strong tree in the ditch.
Whole ones are temporal lobes,
smashed ones pulpy greenish matter.
Chartreuse, I think they call that color.
A noble, intelligent word.
My right foot lands in a cerebral pile.
It stinks and clings to my shoe.

Can I please be done now?
Please?

But two more miles stretch ahead.
Always two more miles.
And my breath is harsh but sure.
I will not die soon.

Sarah Brown

Your Turn

Write a poem in which you recount a period in your life when you felt "too far down" to continue much further. Like Robert Lowell, you should avoid excessive self-pity and allow the concrete details of your poem to convey the experience to your reader.

Because depression is a subject that untrained poets naturally turn to, it has inspired oceans of bad poetry. Most of this writing is bad not because it is insincere, but rather because it is *too* sincere. When you pour your heart out, chances are you will use the first phrases that come to mind. These phrases—like "pour your heart out"—are clichés. They accurately describe how you are feeling, but they make for inferior poetry.

Notice, for instance, how expert Lowell and Sarah are at letting the landscape subtly (and sometimes not so subtly) reflect their moods. For them, the landscape is an objective correlative for their speakers' emotions. **Objective correlative** is a term coined by T. S. Eliot in his 1919 essay "Hamlet and His Problems." Eliot's own explanation of the term is rather obscure, but it has come to mean an object or situation that evokes a particular set of emotions in a reader. When, for example, the squirrel is run over toward the end of Sarah's poem, the squirrel serves effectively as an objective correlative, a concrete representation of the poet's feelings about the harshness of life and the inevitability of death.

Chapter Twenty-Four

Grandparents

In this chapter you will write a poem about one or more of your grandparents. Because not everyone knows or was close to their grandparents, you may end up writing a poem based on family memories, or you may even create fictional characters. Of course your poem might also express your frustration and sorrow at not knowing your grandparents personally.

Mary TallMountain clearly has a strong sense of who her grandmother was. We are not told if Matmiya is the name of the speaker's grandmother or if she is a figure from the pantheon of the Athabascans (TallMountain's people). In either case, Matmiya illustrates the literal and figurative *depth* of the connection between generations. By envisioning her grandmother as a kind of tree-woman whose roots extend "Through fertile earthscapes / Where each layer feeds the next / Into depths immutable," TallMountain emphasizes the importance of her own ancestral heritage. This transformation of a real person into an archetype helps the poet more easily make the point that even when one of our forebears passes away, her "spirit remains / Nourished, / Nourishing [the descendants]."

Matmiya
(for my Grandmother)

I see you sitting
Implanted by roots
Coiled deep from your thighs.
Roots, flesh red, centuries pale.
Hairsprings wound tight
Through fertile earthscapes
Where each layer feeds the next
Into depths immutable.

Though you must rise, must
Move large and slow
When it is time, O my
Gnarled mother-vine, ancient
As vanished ages,
Your spirit remains
Nourished,
Nourishing me.

I see your figure wrapped in skins
Curved into a mound of earth
Holding your rich dark roots.
Matmiya,
I see you sitting.

Mary TallMountain

If you have had a close relationship with your grandparents, you may be hesitant to see them as less than flawless. Certainly, there is no need to become a family muckraker, but do not shy away from details that present your grandparents as real live people. Notice, for instance, how Mary TallMountain uses imagery that suggests an earthiness—"Roots, flesh red, centuries pale" or "Gnarled mother-vine"—that a careless reader might misconstrue as unflattering.

Aside from her attachment to the earth, the other main impression of Matmiya we are left with is her stasis. The opening and closing lines are the same: "I see you sitting." Even when she eventually rises, it will be "large and slow." This image of the grandmother contradicts the one promoted by Anglo popular culture. We expect her to be busy: baking pies, mending clothes, taking care of her husband and grandchildren, cleaning up. Instead, TallMountain gives us a woman whose wisdom is calm and almost impenetrable.

Scott Anderberg's grandfather is similarly stoic. His life has been difficult, "full of hard days / . . . in the field" and memories of war. Indeed, his experiences are so complex that there is "too much there for one wrinkle to hold." Scott knows that he cannot squeeze the diversity of a person's entire life into a single poem.

However, whereas Mary TallMountain relies on a dominant metaphor—the tree—to portray her grandmother, Scott concentrates on a single physical feature of his grandfather: the wrinkles on his face. Scott imagines that each wrinkle represents an important event or person in his grandfather's life. His face is his autobiography: it tells the story of his immigration to America—"of leaning over rails and smelling / salt, of hair whipped by ocean wind"—all the way to his death, when "His Bible was engraved on the troughs / of his eyelids."

Wrinkles

I think they are where
he kept his memories, tucked
tight in the folds of skin on his face.

The long wrinkle below his left
eye held the story of sailing to America.
The story of leaning over rails and smelling
salt, of hair whipped by ocean wind,
of stumbling feet on heaving decks.

An old Indian chief had caught him and
kept him from falling in a train once
when the darkness of a tunnel closed in.
The kind man's bright feathers
terrified him, but they are etched
in the line between his nose and upper lip.

Each of his children are on his forehead.
Each one housed in a separate fold.
John came first. His line is longest, carved
just above the brow and full of hard days
together in the field. Lola is next, above
the left eye. Dot's line is narrow and tight
from so many years of sickness.

The war is a long wrinkle
above his right cheek. It droops
a little, like it's tired, like there is
too much there for one wrinkle to hold.

Only when he laughs does it pull tight
against his face and withdraw
from the heaviness of those days.

His Bible was engraved on the troughs
of his eyelids. His eye sockets deep,
like his faith, and when he left us his eyelids
fluttered closed, just the way it
looked when he thumbed through
the pages of that big book.

Scott Anderberg

Your Turn

Write a poem about one or more of your grandparents. Look for the unexpected. Mary
TallMountain's grandmother reminds her of a tree; Scott Anderberg is fascinated by his
grandfather's wrinkles. Perhaps your grandfather's love of fishing suggests a metaphorical way of depicting him, or the scent of your grandmother's perfume may inspire certain poignant memories of her.

Although this might at first seem like a relatively easy assignment, it does present
some obstacles. Your initial tendency will probably be to generalize and sentimentalize
your grandparents. To avoid that, you might want to begin by freewriting (described in
Chapter 18). Try to jot down as many *specifics* as you can remember. Instead of "She
was a very sweet, loving, caring grandmother," recall specific incidents that make you
feel that way, such as, "I'll never forget the time my bicycle was stolen and my grandmother sold her favorite antique vase to buy me a new ten-speed."

After you have generated sufficient source material and worked it into an appropriate poem, revise carefully. Look for places where you can make your subject more
individual, more real. Delete images and anecdotes that simply mimic the caricatures
we see in greeting cards and television commercials.

Chapter Twenty-Five

Homage to Other Poets

Chapter Twenty-Five asks you to write a poem in homage to another poet. To pay **homage** to someone means to show that person special respect. *Poetry Writing* itself implicitly asks you to pay homage to other poets by modeling your own work on theirs. This assignment simply makes that act the focus of a poem. As noted in the Preface, beginning writers today sometimes feel uncomfortable "copying" the work of earlier poets. It is important to remember, therefore, that this method of honoring by way of imitation was, until recently, considered a crucial aspect of every poet's education.

Denise Levertov's homage is to William Carlos Williams, someone who had an enormous influence on her own aesthetic. Like her mentor, Levertov was not interested in "the bald image" but rather in the secrets of the body and the mind, which are "lodged // among the words, beneath / the skin of image." Both poets looked for beauty

114

in unexpected places; they tried to hear music in "the twang of plucked / catgut"; they found dark riches in "the wily mud."

In the process of naming what she admires in Williams's poetry, Levertov also indicates what she strives for in her own work. In this respect, "Williams: An Essay" serves not only as a tribute, but also as a critical guide to Levertov's past writing and a blueprint for her future poems.

Williams: An Essay

His theme
over and over:

the twang of plucked
catgut
from which struggles
music,

the tufted swampgrass
quicksilvering
dank meadows,

a baby's resolute fury—metaphysic
of appetite and tension.

Not
the bald image, but always—
undulant, elusive, beyond reach
of any dull
staring eye—lodged

among the words, beneath
the skin of image: nerves,
muscles, rivers
of urgent blood, a mind

secret, disciplined, generous and
unfathomable.
                    Over

and over,
his theme
            hid itself and
smilingly reappeared.

> He loved
> persistence—but it must
> be linked to invention: landing
>
> backwards, 'facing
> into the wind's teeth,'
>   to please him.
>
> He loved
> the lotus cup, fragrant
> upon the swaying water, loved
>
> the wily mud
> pressing swart riches into its roots,
>
> and the long stem of connection.
>
> *Denise Levertov*

Levertov pays homage to Williams in form as well as content. Many of his poems look like the one above: they are composed of short lines in short stanzas, with plenty of white space left on the page (see, for example, Chapter 5). Williams believed that much of what happens in a poem—the part that is implied but left unsaid—occurs in this white space. Writing in the style of Williams, Levertov proves that, far from being a hindrance to philosophical thought, his short, insinuating lines can marry theory with a precise description of the physical world.

Not everyone has bought into this notion, however. In fact, during the backlash that inevitably occurs when a great poet dies, Williams was chastised for popularizing the "skinny poem." Critics derided the short lines, the highly imagistic and aphoristic language (an **aphorism** is a succinct, memorable formulation). They insisted that Williams's followers simply described the world without ever actually confronting or thinking about it. These critics declared that Williams's famous dictum, "No ideas but in things," had been shortened by his less thoughtful followers to "No ideas. Period." As her poem makes clear, Levertov disagrees.

In his response to the model poem, Jamie Molitor also writes in the style and addresses the subject matter of one of his writing heroes. Lewis Carroll's "Jabberwocky," which originally appeared in *Through the Looking-Glass,* has long been a favorite of poets. Fans of Carroll love his sense of fantasy and satire and his playfulness with language, especially his use of **neologisms** (newly coined, sometimes meaningless words or phrases). Jamie shares this enthusiasm. He uses Carroll's jingly *abcb* quatrains. And he keeps his tongue firmly in his cheek, taking much of the vocabulary in the poem directly from "Jabberwocky."

To Lewis Carroll

Your jabberwocky makes my mash
  Go challer-chab until it burns.
I lose my millmat every time
  That manxome foe returns.

I stand alone in uffish thought
  To contemplate your work of art.
I wonder if your mind went fash
  Before you rummed flaggart.

Lewis, you maze my abberath
  Each time the toves are in the wabe.
I love how you make the Jubjub birds
  Go chicker or chillabe.

Jamie Molitor

Your Turn

This exercise asks you to write about the work of a poet you admire. However, unlike a critical essay written for a literature class, the poetic "essay" gives you freedom to address any important aspect of that person's work, and it lets you examine the poetry in as creative a fashion as you choose.

Both the theme poem and the student variation employ a form associated with the person to whom they are paying homage. This strategy enables the "junior" poet to duplicate some of the characteristic phrasing and the music of the person who is being honored. Think about your subject. Does the poet often write in a particular form? If so, what is it? If he or she typically uses free verse, what are its qualities? Are the lines long or short? Are they dense with imagery or spartan and plain?

Chapter Twenty-Six

Secret Parents

In James Dickey's "The Celebration" a son sees his parents, but they do not see him. Because it is one-sided, the poet finds this encounter all the more intriguing. Your poem, too, will feature a narrator who secretly follows one or both of his parents and witnesses them acting in an unexpected fashion.

"The Celebration" is set on the midway of a carnival. In the first two stanzas, the speaker wanders along engrossed by the sights: a fire-breathing man, a roller coaster, "the dodgem cars." Then, abruptly and entirely by accident, he sees his parents, who he thought were at home in bed. Instead, they are strolling around like young lovers. His father wins a teddy bear for his mother "on the waning / Whip of his right arm," then the elderly couple boards the Ferris wheel. As the speaker watches it spin, he is transported into a kind of mystic vision that allows him to understand "the whirling impulse / From which [he] had been born."

"The Celebration" gives both the narrator and the reader an opportunity to act as voyeurs. We look over the speaker's shoulder as he discovers new facets of his parents' lives and a new perspective on his own. This combination makes for a nearly irresistible model poem.

The Celebration

All wheels; a man breathed fire,
Exhaling like a blowtorch down the road
And burnt the stripper's gown
Above her moving-barely feet.
A condemned train climbed from the earth
Up stilted nightlights zooming in a track.
I ambled along in that crowd

Between the gambling wheels
At carnival time with the others
Where the dodgem cars shuddered, sparking
On grillwire, each in his vehicle half
In control, half helplessly power-mad
As he was in the traffic that brought him.
No one blazed at me; then I saw

My mother and my father, he leaning
On a dog-chewed cane, she wrapped to the nose
In the fur of exhausted weasels.
I believed them buried miles back
In the country, in the faint sleep
Of the old, and had not thought to be
On this of all nights compelled

To follow where they led, not losing
Sight, with my heart enlarging whenever
I saw his crippled Stetson bob, saw her
With the teddy bear won on the waning
Whip of his right arm. They laughed;
She clung to him; then suddenly
The Wheel of wheels was turning

The colored night around.
They climbed aboard. My God, they rose
Above me, stopped themselves and swayed
Fifty feet up; he pointed
With his toothed cane, and took in

The whole Midway till they dropped,
Came down, went from me, came and went

Faster and faster, going up backward,
Cresting, out-topping, falling roundly.
From the crowd I watched them,
Their gold teeth flashing,
Until my eyes blurred with their riding
Lights, and I turned from the standing
To the moving mob, and went on:

Stepped upon sparking shocks
Of recognition when I saw my feet
Among the others, knowing them given,
Understanding the whirling impulse
From which I had been born,
The great gift of shaken lights,
The being wholly lifted with another,

All this having all and nothing
To do with me. Believers, I have seen
The wheel in the middle of the air
Where old age rises and laughs,
And on Lakewood Midway became
In five strides a kind of loving,
A mortal, a dutiful son.

James Dickey

Biologists and psychologists tell us that our strongest genetic and emotional ties are likely to be with our parents. Whether your own parents are long absent or have been around since your birth, chances are that you have some pretty powerful feelings about them. This chapter allows you to look at your relationship with your mother and/or father from an oblique angle. It frees you up to say more than you might normally say. In essence, it asks you to reverse the usual parent-child dynamic as you become the observer rather than the observed, the judge rather than the judged.

James Dickey learns that he has a stronger connection to his parents than he had imagined. The experience at the carnival teaches him that he is "A mortal, a dutiful son." The student response poem is quite different. Rather than reaffirming the strength of the parent-child bond, the narrator's father turns out to be much less of a role model than his son would have wanted.

Like the narrator in "The Celebration," the son in Charles Jones's "Empress" (named after a riverboat casino in Joliet, Illinois) has prepared himself for a big night out alone. He is ready to get his "swerve on," but instead of finding an anonymous environment in which he can fulfill fantasies of himself as a big-time gambler, he arrives to see his father "looking like a roaring twenties gangster or space-age pimp."

Charles's poem is more lighthearted than Dickey's, yet the speaker clearly feels uncomfortable in the presence of a man who (his son believes) should be preparing for church rather than living it up. The implication, obviously, is that the father is a hypocrite, yet the tone the son chooses to tell the story diverts our attention from a potentially serious falling-out between the two, and focuses instead on the comedy of the situation.

Empress

Ain't this about a . . .
I know he didn't just step up in the place.
Of all the riverboats, of all the nights he had to pick
this one, the night I'm tryin' to get my swerve on.
Look at him, my old man, standing there in the midst
of all the bright lights and degenerate gamblers
with his zoot suit and Dobb hat,
looking like a roaring twenties gangster or space-age pimp.
This ain't my old man,
       the Sunday school teacher,
          the Deacon,
             Mister Morality.
Humph, that's him all right,
strollin' over to the crap table sippin' on a Cognac.
I don't dare say anything to him or risk hearing one of his
sermons.
So I duck behind a slot machine, where I can see him
shaking the dice with hopes of hittin' a seven,
       eleven,
          a point,
             or those runnin' mates
six and eight.
"Poppa need a new pair of shoes!"
I hear him yell before he tosses the dice once more.
I can't believe it!
My old man was hot
       with the seven come eleven
          and back doorin' points
             left and right.
He's hot
and I'm down to my last yard.

He ain't supposed to be here!
Where he should be is somewhere
            preparing a Sunday school lesson,
                  underlining a passage in the Good Book,
                        visiting the sick
or something.
Why is he stealing my joy?
Ain't this about a . . .

Charles Jones

Your Turn

Imagine that you experience what happens to the speakers in James Dickey's and Charles Jones's poems. You are someplace far from home when you suddenly and unexpectedly spot one or both of your parents. As you follow them surreptitiously, they remain unaware of your presence and behave in ways you would never have anticipated.

Answers to the following questions may be relevant: Where does your poem take place? At what time of the night or day? How are your parents behaving differently than they normally do? Does your respect for them increase or diminish as a result of what you see?

Remember that the events in your poem are more than likely made-up. (Charles's poem, for instance, is entirely fabricated.) Moreover, the parents and the child in the poem may well be nothing more than distant likenesses of the real people involved.

Chapter Twenty-Seven

Epistolary Poems

Although there are many hundreds of **epistolary** novels (i.e., novels written in the form of letters) we do not normally think of letter writing as a mode of poetic discourse. Nevertheless, the spontaneity of an epistolary poem, the way it lends itself to story telling and allows the writer to convey odd yet interesting details, makes it a rewarding form, and in this chapter you will write a poem in the guise of a letter.

Richard Hugo's book *31 Letters and 13 Dreams,* which includes "Letter to Ammons," takes advantage of our natural curiosity to know what other people say in their private correspondence to one another. Published in 1977, the book contains letters to many of the most prominent American poets of the time, among them several of the authors in this book: Denise Levertov, Gary Snyder, and William Stafford.

The "Ammons" of this particular poem is A. R. Ammons, winner of a number of major literary prizes and author of many volumes of poetry,

123

including *Corson's Inlet,* which is mentioned in line 18. Although the letter is chatty and intimate, Hugo keeps the range of personal references to a minimum, and those few he subtly explains. Clearly, he is traveling in Italy and has made a temporary home in the town of Maratea. We assume from the context in which she is mentioned that Phyllis is Ammons's wife. And while it helps to know beforehand that Richard Howard is a poet, editor, and powerful literary critic, something of his reputation is nevertheless suggested in the poem.

Letter to Ammons from Maratea

Dear Archie: I hope the boat trip home wasn't long
but isn't any trip on the United States line? I'm trying
a bomber crash poem and I'm working in short lines.
I wish you were here to advise me on the timing.
You time them well. I'm lost without that harsh, often
too booming voice across the page. It snowed last night
in the mountains and I consider that un-Italian.
What a bust Italy was for you. Remember when someone
asked you what you'd do in Rome, you said, walk along
the Tiber and look at weeds. You should have come here.
Phyllis speaks Italian and you'd have gotten along.
The people here are honest and the setting—Lord, the rise
of stone mountains out of the sea and the sea clearer
than gin. When it storms, the sea is blue milk,
and you can look at the little things, not just weeds
but the old sepia prints of dead men ringed with flowers
and the short silver fish they catch in the Mediterranean.
Like Corson's Inlet, it says, I say, come. I hope
Richard Howard accepts your invitation to spend time
with you and Phyllis on the ocean. What good company
he is, except he seldom is because he's always working.
The only bad thing here is, I'm lonely. For three months
I haven't spoken English to anyone, and my Italian
gets by only because the Italians are *simpatici.*
I'm wrapping up the book and going soon to London.
I've sent Richard the poems and the table of contents
and he says, that's it. What better guarantee?
I'll take the train, like the man in one of my poems.
I think I'll never see this again. But then I found it
like we find all things, by lucky accident, sometimes
not so lucky, and I'll carry it with me like a man
carries a dream of curved giant women who say, come
and beckon to us, come, and who are never there
and never go away. Your Neapolitan Buddy, Dick.

Richard Hugo

Remember that while this is a letter, it is also a *poem:* lines are more important than sentences. Therefore, you should try to end lines on strong, important words rather than articles or prepositions. Use enjambment creatively. You should also be aware of rhythm. Richard Hugo makes his letter more recognizably poetic by writing in iambic hexameter. In other words, he has six feet per line, with a **rising meter,** that is, the syllables in each foot go from unstressed to stressed (a **falling meter** moves from stressed to unstressed syllables).

While Kim Pinnow writes in free verse, she gives the poem some structure by organizing it into three-line stanzas, with the first and third lines slightly indented. Like Hugo's "Letter to Ammons," Kim's "Strawberry Stationery" refers to a specific incident—a memorable night at an Alabama tattoo parlor. And she draws our attention to the stationery on which she's writing. Even though our eyes cannot literally "see" the green vines on the red paper, we can imagine them, and her description gives the letter an added sense of **verisimilitude** (the quality of appearing real or true).

Strawberry Stationery

Have you noticed I am writing
on the stationery you
gave me in September?

Just looking at it reminds me
of that night in Alabama.
I can still hear the sound,

the buzzing of the needle
as it touched my skin.
The red ink looked like blood.

I told you it didn't hurt
that bad, knowing you
would back out if it did.

I can remember your white
face as I saw the black
etched across your hip.

What a way to bond
our friendship, a last high
school ambition, I guess.

We will have these reminders
long after the green vines
and red fruit on this paper fade.

Kim Pinnow

Your Turn

Write a poem to a friend in the form of a letter. As you write, remember that the most interesting letter poems are those that are, like Hugo's and Kim's, addressed to a real friend and use real facts from your life. Of course, you will also have to take into account the secondary audience looking over the shoulder of your primary reader. Do not be *too* revealing. The two poets above manage this balancing act with skill and grace. They avoid embarrassing their correspondents (although Kim comes awfully close), yet they include enough tantalizing details to make us want to read on.

As always, if it will make for a better poem, it is perfectly all right to invent both a letter writer and a reader. In fact, if you live a fairly mundane life, it might be preferable. A memorable poem excuses just about any well-meaning lie.

Chapter Twenty-Eight

Metaphors for Love

Throughout this book, poets have been using metaphorical language, just as you have no doubt been using it in your responses. This chapter will put that special type of language in the spotlight. As you probably already know, an **analogy** indicates a correspondence between two unlike things. Because poets are always looking for hidden similarities to help them make sense of the world, they frequently employ words or phrases that are normally used to describe one thing and transfer that description to something else. If this comparison or analogy is implied—"Your face is the sunshine"—we use the term **metaphor.** If we use the words "like" or "as" to make the comparison—"Your face is like the sunshine" or "Your face is as bright as the sunshine"—the analogy is called a **simile.**

Your assignment for this chapter is to write a poem that uses bizarre similes and/or metaphors. To make things even more interesting, the poem you write will be about love. This may sound like

127

a slap in the face of romance, but think about it: most of us have great difficulty expressing our truest affection in terms that are not, upon reflection, downright silly.

This is probably because innovative love poetry is so difficult to write. If the reader is not the writer's beloved, he may well find the lover's language exorbitant, ridiculous, and clichéd. Just consider a few of the banalities we associate with courtship. Lovers address each other using nicknames like "honey bunch" and "sweetie pie." They "burn with love" at the beginning of an affair and "drown in tears" when it is over.

Kenneth Koch solves this problem in "To You" by using wild, improbably specific similes to let his beloved know how much he cares for her. The result is both comic ("I am crazier than shirttails / In the wind, when you're near") and strangely touching ("I love you as the sunlight leads the prow / Of a ship"). If the resulting poem seems less heartfelt than the greeting card verse most lovelorn people pen, it nevertheless makes for a much more intriguing piece of literature.

To You

I love you as a sheriff searches for a walnut
That will solve a murder case unsolved for years
Because the murderer left it in the snow beside a window
Through which he saw her head, connecting with
Her shoulders by a neck, and laid a red
Roof in her heart. For this we live a thousand years;
For this we love, and we live because we love, we are not
Inside a bottle, thank goodness! I love you as a
Kid searches for a goat: I am crazier than shirttails
In the wind, when you're near, a wind that blows from
The big blue sea, so shiny so deep and so unlike us;
I think I am bicycling across an Africa of green and white
        fields
Always, to be near you, even in my heart
When I'm awake, which swims, and also I believe that you
Are trustworthy as the sidewalk which leads me to
The place where I again think of you, a new
Harmony of thoughts! I love you as the sunlight leads the
        prow
Of a ship which sails
From Hartford to Miami, and I love you
Best at dawn, when even before I am awake the sun
Receives me in the questions which you always pose.

Kenneth Koch

In his 1936 book *Philosophy of Rhetoric,* American literary critic I. A. Richards coined the terms **tenor** for the subject to which a metaphor is applied and **vehicle** for the metaphoric term itself. Because poetry is so full of metaphors, you may find these terms useful as you discuss your own and other people's poems. In the opening passage of "To You," for example, the tenor is the speaker's love for his darling. The vehicles are "a sheriff search[ing] for a walnut" and "a / Kid search[ing] for a goat." By definition, the vehicle and tenor must differ from each other, but these differences are so huge and so preposterous that it is clear the poet wants nothing to do with traditional sentiment.

Katy Montgomery echoes this effect nicely. The first line of her poem uses "arms" as the tenor and "the words of the Gettysburg Address" as the vehicle, hardly a predictable combination. Wisely, Katy retains a tongue-in-cheek awareness of her exaggerations. She uses similes drawn from a wide range of subject matter: history ("the Gettysburg Address"), domestic life ("clothes in a dryer," "the phone in the middle of dinner," "milk blown through a straw"), sports ("bluer than Boston in a World Series") and consumer culture ("More than the Rabbit loves Trix"). The effect of this mélange of references is to make it seem as though the speaker's beloved is on her mind no matter where she is or what she is doing. Where there is love, Katy seems to imply, there is metaphor.

"Your arms are stronger than the words . . ."

Your arms are stronger than the words of the Gettysburg
    Address.
Yet soft and warm as clothes in a dryer.

And your eyes—bluer than Boston in a World Series,
Deeper than the stack of papers on my desk.

Your voice rings like the phone in the middle of dinner,
It bubbles in me like milk blown through a straw.

How much do I love you?
    More than a fire loves oxygen.
    More than the mailman loves Sundays.
    More than the Rabbit loves Trix.

Katy Montgomery

Your Turn

Follow Kenneth Koch's and Katy Montgomery's lead and write a love poem that uses similes and/or metaphors that are outlandish yet still somehow appropriate. If you do not currently have a significant someone, make up a lover. Whether or not the person is real, for the purposes of this exercise you will obviously have to assume that your beloved has a sense of humor.

Let your imagination go crazy. If you think the object of your affection has eyes that sparkle like something bright, the first comparison that may come to mind is a diamond. Clearly, that cliché won't do. Make a list of other things that sparkle: ice, glass, champagne, fool's gold, the plastic wrapper on a new CD, a butter knife taken from the dishwasher and held up to the morning sunlight pouring through the kitchen window. Were you to establish a hierarchy of vehicles for your tenor, the first two would be weak, the second two slightly better, and the final two the most appropriate for this assignment.

Chapter Twenty-Nine

Repetition with a Difference

As any musician will tell you, repetition is an essential part of music. From the latest pop song on the radio to a Mozart symphony, a musical idea gains power when it reappears later in the same work. Your poem this time will not be set to music, but it will follow a very particular pattern of theme and variations.

Donald Justice's "Variations for Two Pianos" is a modification of the **villanelle,** a French form that consists of five tercets and a final quatrain. The first and third lines (A^1 and A^2) of the first tercet recur alternately in all subsequent tercets and become the final couplet in the quatrain. The rhyme scheme in the tercets is *aba,* and the second lines of all stanzas rhyme with each other. The quatrain rhymes *abaa.* Overall, a villanelle might look like this in outline: $A^1 bA^2\ abA^1\ abA^2\ abA^1\ abA^2\ abA^1A^2.$

Justice's simplified version proceeds as follows: The first two lines, *A* ("There is no music now in all Arkansas") and *B* ("Higgins is gone, taking both his pianos"), alternate as the last lines in the four tercets. The first lines of each tercet, *c*, all rhyme with each other ("away" with "Conway," and so on). *A* becomes its own one-line stanza at the end of the poem. Although this may sound complicated at first, it will become clear as you read. Just by looking at "Variations," you should be able to discern the fairly simple pattern: *AB cdA ceB cfA cgB A.*

Variations for Two Pianos

There is no music now in all Arkansas.
Higgins is gone, taking both his pianos.

Movers dismantled the instruments, away
Sped the vans. The first detour untuned the strings.
There is no music now in all Arkansas.

Up Main Street, past the cold shopfronts of Conway,
The brash, self-important brick of the college,
Higgins is gone, taking both his pianos.

Warm evenings, the windows open, he would play
Something of Mozart's for his pupils, the birds.
There is no music now in all Arkansas.

How shall the mockingbird mend her trill, the jay
His eccentric attack, lacking a teacher?
Higgins is gone, taking both his pianos.

There is no music now in all Arkansas.

Donald Justice

Donald Justice, himself a piano player, uses music very effectively in "Variations for Two Pianos." The poem repeats two lines, the themes, but each time in the context of a new stanza, the variations. Like the calls of the mockingbird and jay, snippets of birdsong in warm evening air, the two lines keep returning without becoming annoying. Indeed, for such a short poem, and one so insistent on repetition, it is vital both that the reiterated lines are both striking in themselves and that they can be used in a variety of situations.

Jamie Molitor's two recurring lines—"The meatloaf just got burned" and "We'll be going out for dinner"—live up to that standard, although Jamie's "Meatloaf" takes a much more lighthearted approach to repetition with a difference. The interplay between the speaker's desire to go out for Italian food and the sad fate of his mother's meatloaf makes for some real comedy. Note how Jamie manipulates the form, like a master stand-up comedian, to wring every laugh he can get from the situation. In addition, Jamie allows himself a little freedom to modify the original. In his variation, it is the first two lines that always rhyme with each other ("reeks" with "beeps," etc.), rather than, as in the Justice poem, the first line of each tercet.

The meatloaf just got burned.
We'll be going out for dinner.

Meatloaf

The air around us reeks,
the smoke detector beeps.
The meatloaf just got burned.

It's far too black to eat,
and it doesn't look like meat.
We'll be going out for dinner.

Spaghetti is my favorite dish.
Mom's meatloaf sucks—I got my wish.
The meatloaf just got burned.

The new gas stove is my salvation,
Cossetta's is our destination.
We'll be going out for dinner.

The meatloaf just got burned.

Jamie Molitor

Your Turn

Try a poem of your own using Donald Justice's version of the villanelle. Look for a subject that lends itself to repetition with a difference, one in which the repeated lines can take on a slightly new meaning each time they reappear.

Because your poem is likely to succeed or fail based on the flexibility of the word or phrase you repeat, choose carefully. The first idea that comes into your head may not be the best one, and if a phrase you thought would work sputters after a few lines, do not hesitate to use another one.

After you write down the two repeating lines, try to think through your poem before you actually write it: Are the lines sufficiently adaptable? Can you envision the scenario in which they will occur? Will reiteration of entire lines emphasize the situation's sadness (as in Justice's poem) or its comedy (as in Jamie's)? Or, alternatively, will the setting of the poem only make the repeating lines seem unnecessary?

Chapter Thirty

Café Life

Over the last couple of centuries, few hangouts have been as appealing to poets as cafés. They gather in these convivial places to discuss the events of the day, to argue with each other about poetry, to read, to think, to fall in and out of love. Sometimes the café seems like a world unto itself, one worthy of the sort of attention this chapter's poem will give it.

Allen Ginsberg was a great aficionado of café life. However, in "Café in Warsaw," Ginsberg relinquishes his more familiar haunts in San Francisco and New York for one in Poland. The poem provides us with a vivid portrait of a surprisingly bohemian setting in an Eastern Bloc city at the height of the Cold War. The girls have "scarred faces, black stockings thin eyebrows," the boys wear "little chin beards." They sit together kissing, chatting, smoking, "reading the art journals" as they wait "for the slow waitress to prepare red hot tea."

Admittedly, the inhabitants of the café all seem like spectres to the poet; their country's history has been tragic, their own lives less than ideal. Yet Ginsberg implies that *because of* the harsh realities outside, life in the café is more romantic, more stylish, more *important* than the "real" world could ever be.

Café in Warsaw

These spectres resting on plastic stools
leather-gloved spectres flitting thru the coffeehouse one hour
spectre girls with scarred faces, black stockings thin eyebrows
spectre boys blond hair combed neat over the skull little chin
    beards
new spectres talking intensely crowded together over black
    shiny tables late afternoon
the sad soprano of history chanting thru a hi-fidelity
    loudspeaker
—perspective walls & windows 18th century down New
    World Avenue to Sigmund III column'd
sword upraised watching over Polish youth & centuries—
O Polish spectres what've you suffered since Chopin wept
    into his romantic piano
old buildings rubbed down, gaiety of all night parties under
    the air bombs,
first screams of the vanishing ghetto—Workmen step thru
    prewar pink-blue bedroom walls demolishing sunny
    ruins—
Now spectres gather to kiss hands, girls kiss lip to lip, red
    witch-hair from Paris
& fine gold watches—sit by the yellow wall with a large
    brown briefcase—
to smoke three cigarettes with thin black ties and nod heads
    over a new movie—
spectres Christ and your bodies be with you for this hour
    while you're young
in postwar heaven stained with the sweat of Communism,
    your loves and your white smooth cheekskin soft in the
    glance of each other's eye.
O spectres how beautiful your clam shaven faces, your pale
    lipstick scarves, your delicate heels,
how beautiful your absent gaze, legs crossed alone at table
    with long eyelashes,
how beautiful your patient love together sitting reading the
    art journals—
how beautiful your entrance thru the velvet-curtained door,
    laughing into the overcrowded room,

how you wait in your hats, measure the faces, and turn and
    depart for an hour,
or meditate at the bar, waiting for the slow waitress to
    prepare red hot tea, minute by minute
standing still as hours ring in churchbells, as years pass and
    you will remain in Novy Swiat,
how beautiful you press your lips together, sigh forth smoke
    from your mouth, rub your hands
or lean together laughing to notice this wild haired madman
    who sits weeping among you a stranger.

April 10, 1965

Allen Ginsberg

One aspect of "Café in Warsaw" that is immediately noticeable is its extremely long lines. Ginsberg seems intent on cramming in as much material as possible, so much so that several of the lines spill over past the right margin and must be indented when they wrap around.

Poet Charles Olson, an early influence on Ginsberg, said that the length of the line should depend on a poet's breath. Ginsberg generally agreed. If that is the case, American poets like Ginsberg, Olson, Walt Whitman, and C. K. Williams must be long-winded indeed. Others, like William Carlos Williams, would have to be considered positively asthmatic.

To find out if this line-breath connection helps you with your own work, try an experiment. Read your poem for this chapter aloud with your breathing in mind. If one normal breath equals one line, should your lines be longer or shorter? Tinker with the lines to see if they are improved by this new method of composition.

Kelly Cannon has definitely benefited from a careful attention to lineation. Each phrase can be spoken comfortably in a modest but healthy breath. Of her poem, Kelly Cannon writes: "I spend a lot of time in the campus coffee house discussing current campus politics, philosophy, and whatnot. That place and the people I see are so important to me. But I always wonder about one of the workers there. What does he think when he hears us all speculating about the universe and our place in it? I wonder what his life is like apart from this place." Kelly's unrelenting curiosity inspires her to write her conjectures down in the form of a fine poem.

Ode to the Boy Behind the Counter in Coffee Dregs

Oh, Coffee Boy, with your hat backward,
I love it when you clean the pots out
at the end of the night.
I know you're secretly wondering
how much is in the tip jar.
And I know you'll walk home smiling,
thinking, "They like me!"

I bet you wish the dishes were clean
so you could blow this joint
and hitch a ride to the next deep conversation.

And yet I see a certain solitude in your eyes that I enjoy.

When you're here alone
before the hustle and bustle
of intellectualism begins,
do you turn up the music and boogie,
or just tap your foot quietly,
pretending to study anatomy?

Kelly Cannon

Your Turn

Write your own poem about café life. You may even want to take a field trip—with pen and paper, of course. Look for interesting people and speculate about who they are and why they are sharing café life with you. Is there anyone in the café you would not expect to see? What are they wearing? What are they talking about? What other sounds are present? What smells do you notice? What does the coffee taste like? What sort of artwork, if any, is hanging on the walls? If the café has windows, what do you see outside? Does the scene outside have any relation to what is going on in the café?

Chapter Thirty-One

Current Events

Frank O'Hara claimed to have picked up the newspaper and jotted down the lines of the following poem on his way to a reading. Whether or not his account is entirely accurate, the result was nevertheless a funny, memorable poem. In this chapter you are asked to make a similar effort to transform news into poetry by flipping through a newspaper until a headline leaps out and demands, "Write about me."

O'Hara's "Poem" begins with an opening hook: "Lana Turner has collapsed!" *Why? How? When?* we want to know, but the poet leaves us in suspense and instead begins talking about the weather and the traffic that hindered his progress as he made his way toward the unidentified person he is addressing.

Suddenly, halfway through the poem, O'Hara repeats the headline, this time in all capital letters. Yet rather than remarking on her fate, he contrasts the weather in New York with that in Southern

California. Then he pauses to compare his own behavior with that of the film star. His conclusion—"I have been to lots of parties / and acted perfectly disgraceful / but I never actually collapsed"—is so unexpected, and yet so in character, that we cannot help but smile at the pinball train of thought that brings him to the wonderful final line.

Poem

Lana Turner has collapsed!
I was trotting along and suddenly
it started raining and snowing
and you said it was hailing
but hailing hits you on the head
hard so it was really snowing and raining
and I was in such a hurry
to meet you but the traffic
was acting exactly like the sky
and suddenly I see a headline
LANA TURNER HAS COLLAPSED!
There is no snow in Hollywood
there is no rain in California
I have been to lots of parties
and acted perfectly disgraceful
but I never actually collapsed
oh Lana Turner we love you get up

Frank O'Hara

The word **style** is used throughout this book to mean the distinctive way that a writer has of expressing him or herself in poetry. Everything from tone and diction to syntax and use of metaphor contribute to a writer's style.

We can also, like classical rhetoricians, divide style into high, middle, and low. Assuming that the example in this chapter is relatively characteristic of his work overall, we might conclude that Frank O'Hara's style is somewhere between middle and low. Certainly he is witty, but the garrulous tone of "Poem" is nowhere as eloquent as that of, say, W. H. Auden's "Lullaby" or Marianne Moore's "The Steeple-Jack." Even free verse poems like Rita Dove's "Adolescence—I" and Elizabeth Bishop's "Questions of Travel" seem to be the result of much more careful forethought than O'Hara's piece.

Yet if O'Hara's language seems much closer to that of poets like Kenneth Koch and Gerald Locklin, writers who cherish the offhand and the colloquial, he cannot be said be writing in a truly low style. At their extreme, such poems not only sound like everyday speech at its most careless, they may also be full of sexual remarks and profanity (not the sort of work you are likely to find in a textbook).

Niki Coate's style and subject matter are much more serious than O'Hara's. The incident described took place in Chicago in 1998 and received national attention. A young man was hit in a drive-by shooting. Afraid of legal repercussions, his friends left him across the street from the hospital. Unfortunately, workers in the emergency room believed that they might be sued if they transported the injured person from where he lay. Instead, they left him there while they called for an ambulance. In the interim, the boy died.

Niki handles all this information with great economy. The poem's title, "Emergency Room Door," focuses on the barrier between the young man and the medical attention he needs. And Nikki's deft rhymes ensure that the tragedy is compressed into rhythmic, memorable language.

Emergency Room Door

A basketball court in the city
A kid that was just in a game
A shooting that started the ending
A bullet that didn't take names

The friends who were frightened of trouble
The doctor who seemed not to care
The door that could have been opened
The teen who could have been spared

Niki Coate

Your Turn

Pick up a copy of your local paper and write a poem about the first item that catches your eye. Do not labor over it. If the poem does not come quickly and naturally, choose another article or come back to this exercise later.

Note that the subject of your poem need not be world-changing. In fact, chances are that a story like the one Niki writes about will make for a better poem than one focusing on arms buildup in the Middle East. That is because, unless you are an expert in foreign policy, you will be much more familiar with the situation closer to home. Moreover, as O'Hara's poem demonstrates, the subject of the story may well be one that triggers your sense of humor.

Chapter Thirty-Two

Rethinking Sports

"Autumn Begins in Martin's Ferry, Ohio" has several themes: the despair of the working class, the inability of men and women to communicate, the sorrows of parenthood. The poem also looks at the way these issues are transformed by sports. James Wright's perspective on football is much more reflective than the one we are used to hearing in the nightly newscasts and on the sports page of the newspaper. Yet the very fact that he is able to resee his subject from an unusual viewpoint makes his poem memorable. Your poem, too, should rethink a particular sport and recast it in surprising new terms.

Football, which many people would consider America's national sport, is a problematic subject for a poem. On the one hand, it is an easy target: the societally sanctioned violence, which is one of the game's chief attractions, might be said to excuse, or even encourage, brutality off the field. On the other hand, sports, especially amateur sports, also offer opportunities for young men and women to test and strengthen their minds and bodies, and sporting events allow families and friends to come together to celebrate this athleticism and to bond with like-minded people.

Those who think of high school football as a battle between valiant warriors will obviously object to James Wright's portrayal of the sport. He depicts the men as impotent has-beens—gray-faced and "ruptured"—who live vicariously through their sons. Yet there is clearly some truth in Wright's depiction. Anyone who has ever been to such an event will recognize the sense of pride and desperation that is obvious both on the gridiron and in the crowd.

Autumn Begins in Martin's Ferry, Ohio

In the Shreve High football stadium,
I think of Polacks nursing long beers in Tiltonsville,
And gray faces of Negroes in the blast furnace at Benwood,
And the ruptured night watchman of Wheeling Steel,
Dreaming of heroes.

All the proud fathers are ashamed to go home.
Their women cluck like starved pullets,
Dying for love.

Therefore,
Their sons grow suicidally beautiful
At the beginning of October,
And gallop terribly against each other's bodies.

James Wright

As noted in the book's appendix, James Wright was among the many American poets who came of age in the late forties and fifties. These poets were trained in traditional English prosody: they wrote carefully metered verse that often made use of elaborate rhyme schemes. By the 1960s, however, following the example of Robert Lowell's *Life Studies,* Wright and others adopted a much looser form. Wright's lines often move back and forth, from very long to very short; yet each line break can be justified. The longest line in the poem, "And gray faces of Negroes in the blast furnace at Benwood," gives us a vivid description of people and place. The shortest line, which consists of the single adverb "Therefore," makes us pause, preparing us for the author's leap of logic in the final stanza.

As you write your own poetry, you may want to take advantage of this freedom to break lines wherever it seems necessary to do so. But be careful. Lines broken willy-nilly, which seem to have no reason for stopping where they do, will probably undermine your reader's confidence in your technique and your seriousness as a poet.

Clearly, alternating long and short lines is inappropriate for a poem like Katy Montgomery's "fusion," which describes a sport where grace and economy of motion are essential. Consequently, Katy's lines are short and tight. In order to convey a sense of rapid, spinning motion, she has centered the poem. Moreover, she has abandoned end punctuation to give the poem the fluidity she associates with ice-skating. Finally, she uses an *abcb* rhyme scheme to help give her reader a feeling of the elegance the best skaters exhibit. Like a centrifuge, revolving faster and faster, the poem and the skater blend together "Alloy of elements / sport, art" until they unite in a whole that will win the judges' approval.

Alloy of elements
ice, steel
Rink of catharsis
breathe, feel

Strength of a rocket
lift, heighten
Grace of a dustrag
polish, brighten

Stack the program
shuffle, deal
Fish for judges
cast and reel

Landing an axel
toepick, down
Play to the audience
flirt and clown

Compete for first
loop, triple throw
Translate music
interpret, show

Canvas of motion
soar, dart
Alloy of elements
sport, art

Katy Montgomery

fusion

Your Turn

Compose a poem that looks at a particular sport from an unusual angle. Do not choose a sport you know nothing about (you may have to do some research if you are not a big sports fan). You should be familiar enough with the sport that your readers have to respect your opinions even if they disagree with them. Katy, for instance, has skated since she was a child. By confidently using terms like "axel," "toepick," and "triple throw," she unobtrusively lets her readers know that she has a working knowledge of figure skating.

Another word of warning: sportswriting is one of the great bastions of clichés in the English language. Therefore, it is vital that if, for instance, you write about the Olympics, you refrain from "going for the gold." Instead, try to formulate new phrases that we do not normally associate with sports. Make comparisons that will leave your reader smiling and thinking: *I wonder why no one ever thought of that before?*

Chapter Thirty-Three

Rewriting Fairy Tales

One school of thought argues that the only thing writers ever really write about is other people's writing. Whether or not that is the case, there is no doubt that responding to and updating an earlier piece of literature can be rewarding. This chapter's assignment encourages you to do that updating in the form of a poem that rewrites and reenvisions a fairy tale.

Once you begin thinking about the possibilities inherent in rewriting fairy tales, you may become as excited about the idea as Anne Sexton, who wrote an entire book, *Transformations* (1971), with that theme. Among the stories she updates are "Snow White and the Seven Dwarfs," "Rumpelstiltskin," "Rapunzel," "Little Red Riding Hood," "Hansel and Gretel," "Sleeping Beauty," and "Cinderella," which appears below. One of the advantages of retelling a narrative like "Cinderella" is that your audience already knows how it is *supposed* to go. The fun is derived from

145

taking the plot in unexpected directions and reshaping the characters to your own ends.

For all its playfulness, however, Anne Sexton's poem is an angry one. She resents the way women are treated as objects to be manipulated. She describes the prince's ball as "a marriage market." The final stanza of the poem—in which she clarifies that "happily ever after" really means living "like two dolls in a museum case"—illustrates her bitterness at the disparity between what we are told about romance as children and what we learn later in life.

Cinderella

You always read about it:
the plumber with twelve children
who wins the Irish Sweepstakes.
From toilets to riches.
That story.

Or the nursemaid,
some luscious sweet from Denmark
who captures the oldest son's heart.
From diapers to Dior.
That story.

Or a milkman who serves the wealthy,
eggs, cream, butter, yogurt, mild,
the white truck like an ambulance,
who goes into real estate
and makes a pile.
From homogenized to martinis at lunch.

Or the charwoman
who is on the bus when it cracks up
and collects enough from the insurance.
From mops to Bonwit Teller.
That story.

Once
the wife of a rich man was on her deathbed
and she said to her daughter Cinderella:
Be devout. Be good. Then I will smile
down from heaven in the seam of a cloud.
The man took another wife who had
two daughters, pretty enough
but with hearts like blackjacks.
Cinderella was their maid.

She slept on the sooty hearth each night
and walked around looking like Al Jolson.
Her father brought presents home from town,
jewels and gowns for the other women
but the twig of a tree for Cinderella.
She planted that twig on her mother's grave
and it grew to a tree where a white dove sat.
Whenever she wished for anything the dove
would drop it like an egg upon the ground.
The bird is important, my dears, so heed him.

Next came the ball, as you all know.
It was a marriage market.
The prince was looking for a wife.
All but Cinderella were preparing
and gussying up for the big event.
Cinderella begged to go too.
Her stepmother threw a dish of lentils
into the cinders and said: Pick them
up in an hour and you shall go.
The white dove brought all his friends;
all the warm wings of the fatherland came,
and picked up the lentils in a jiffy.
No, Cinderella, said the stepmother,
you have no clothes and cannot dance.
That's the way with stepmothers.

Cinderella went to the tree at the grave
and cried forth like a gospel singer:
Mama! Mama! My turtledove,
send me to the prince's ball!
The bird dropped down a golden dress
and delicate little gold slippers.
Rather a large package for a simple bird.
So she went. Which is no surprise.
Her stepmother and sisters didn't
recognize her without her cinder face
and the prince took her hand on the spot
and danced with no other the whole day.

As nightfall came she thought she'd better
get home. The prince walked her home
and she disappeared into the pigeon house
and although the prince took an axe and broke

it open she was gone. Back to her cinders.
These events repeated themselves for three days.
However on the third day the prince
covered the palace steps with cobbler's wax
and Cinderella's gold shoe stuck upon it.
Now he would find whom the shoe fit
and find his strange dancing girl for keeps.
He went to their house and the two sisters
were delighted because they had lovely feet.

The eldest went into a room to try the slipper on
but her big toe got in the way so she simply
sliced it off and put on the slipper.
The prince rode away with her until the white dove
told him to look at the blood pouring forth.
That is the way with amputations.
They don't just heal up like a wish.
The other sister cut off her heel
but the blood told as blood will.
The prince was getting tired.
He began to feel like a shoe salesman.
But he gave it one last try.
This time Cinderella fit into the shoe
like a love letter into its envelope.

At the wedding ceremony
the two sisters came to curry favor
and the white dove pecked their eyes out.
Two hollow spots were left
like soup spoons.

Cinderella and the prince
lived, they say, happily ever after,
like two dolls in a museum case
never bothered by diapers or dust,
never arguing over the timing of an egg,
never telling the same story twice,
never getting a middle-aged spread,
their darling smiles pasted on for eternity.
Regular Bobbsey Twins.
That story.

Anne Sexton

As you read through "Cinderella," you will be struck by the many anachronisms Sexton uses. An **anachronism** is something that appears out of its proper historical time. For instance, early movies about dinosaurs often featured cavemen. Since dinosaurs had become extinct long before people emerged, the cavemen were anachronistic. Anachronisms like this are awkward and embarrassing. Yet when it is employed artfully this device can add a great deal of verve to a work of literature. Anne Sexton is especially good at using anachronistic similes: "two daughters, pretty enough, / but with hearts like blackjacks," she writes. And: "Cinderella went to the tree at the grave / and cried forth like a gospel singer." And, later: "[The Prince] began to feel like a shoe salesman." Sexton's anachronisms add humor to "Cinderella" and make the old story feel more contemporary.

Of her variation on the model poem, Katy Montgomery says, "When I thought of Goldilocks, I thought of her coloring her hair, and decided to start writing. The individual ideas just kept coming as I was writing it." While she shares a sense of play with Sexton, Katy's poem isn't nearly as acrimonious. Her Goldilocks is more concerned with having fun. Like the fairy tale character, this Goldilocks is indolent ("she had dropped her aerobics / class three months ago and had a natural / affinity for beef jerky") and curious. However, the traditional details have all been modernized, and this is where Katy makes the old story come to life.

The Story of Goldilocks (a.k.a Cocoatresses)

One day Goldilocks—or Cocoatresses
as you may remember her from the days
before she had her hair colored—was
dragging herself through the nature preserve . . .
you try finding one bear, let alone three,
somewhere else these days. Originally,
she had been frolicking through the nature
preserve, like any other good heroine
would do, but she had dropped her aerobics
class three months ago and had a natural
affinity for beef jerky, so her doctor
warned against any sort of prolonged
frolicking. She had just about hit the
wall when she happened upon a quaint
little cabin—and with quaint little
cabins being rare these days, she stepped in
to catch her breath. Now, I know you're
imagining all sorts of chairs, beds, and
porridges, but let me tell ya . . . get real.
Would you risk all sorts of breaking and entering
charges for some lousy oatmeal? I think not.
First thing, Goldilocks did was pour herself
a Jose Cuervo Pre-Mixed Margarita.
Feeling the need to bust a move, she put

her Chumbawumba album on the five-disk
CD changer. She then went outside and
dove into the in-ground pool—well, actually
she did a sort of a belly flop, but
that's really beside the point. It was
about that time that the three bears returned
from their trip to the beach. Having put
on only SPF 10 sunblock, and not
SPF 15, they were all badly
burnt and in a rather grizzly mood.
Papa Bear went straight for the liquor
cabinet and was not happy with the
results. "Someone's been drinking my Jose
Cuervo Pre-Mixed Margaritas," he roared,
"and there's not a drop left." Mama Bear was
similarly angry when she went to
put her Barry Manilow CD on.
"Someone's been messing with my stereo,"
she cried, "and they're playing Chumbawumba!"
Baby Bear, feeling he had not gotten
quite enough solar radiation for
one day, was just about to jump in the
pool when he noticed the cement around
it was wet. "Someone's been swimming in my
pool," he hollered, and upon seeing a
blonde head (with brown roots) surfacing in the
deep end, he added, "and there she is!"
At that point, all three bears ran over
to the pool and cannonballed in, but
unfortunately for them, their combined
weight was enough to create an enormous
wave that sent Goldilocks surfing back
into the nature preserve. Goldilocks
continued along the path, her mind
haunted by the fear that they had enough
evidence to make a positive ID,
and also remorseful over the loss of
her Chumbawumba CD. She needn't
have worried, though. After contemplating
the situation, the three bears reasoned
that Goldilocks was mentally disturbed
because she had not fully gotten over
her traumatic childhood. They decided
not to press charges.

Katy Montgomery

Your Turn

Write a poem that updates a fairy tale. Follow the original fairy tale's basic story, but let your imagination run wild with the details. Ironically, as both "Cinderella" and "The Story of Goldilocks" demonstrate, the more you incorporate references to your own time, the more timeless the fairy tale will become.

In his afterword to *The Complete Grimm's Fairy Tales,* Joseph Campbell writes that the "world of magic [in fairy tales] is symptomatic of fevers deeply burning in the psyche: permanent presences, desires, fears, ideals, potentialities, that have glowed in the nerves, hummed in the blood, baffled the senses, since the beginning." Your poem, too, should try to tap into these deeply felt and essential human impulses.

Chapter Thirty-Four

Disguises

When soldiers go into combat, they usually wear some form of camouflage to help them blend in with their surroundings. This makes sense. They know that if they stand out too much, they will be shot and killed. The camouflage you or your character don in this chapter may not be as literal as that worn by an infantryman, but it should be just as effective. The assignment is to remember or imagine a time when you put on a disguise and entered potentially hostile territory.

Gary Snyder's "I Went into the Maverick Bar" presents the reader with a potential battleground between two cultures, the straight and the hip. The poem originally appeared in Snyder's 1974 Pulitzer Prize-winning volume *Turtle Island,* and like many of the poems in that book, it contrasts the "short-haired" world of Middle America with the world of poets, environmentalists and other nonconformists.

Yet despite the fact that Snyder clearly favors the latter community over the former, he is not so closed-minded that he cannot appreciate the innocent roughhousing of his fellow countrymen. For Snyder, his disguise is a way to get closer to the truth about people who would normally ostracize him. "America—your stupidity," he writes, after spending time with cowboys and small-town waitresses. "I could almost love you again."

I Went into the Maverick Bar

I went into the Maverick Bar
In Farmington, New Mexico,
And drank double shots of bourbon
                    backed with beer.
My long hair was tucked up under a cap
I'd left the earring in the car.

Two cowboys did horseplay
                    by the pool tables,
A waitress asked us
                    where are you from?
A country-and-western band began to play
"We don't smoke Marijuana in Muskokie"
And with the next song,
                    a couple began to dance.

They held each other like in High School dances
                    in the fifties;
I recalled when I worked in the woods
                    and the bars of Madras, Oregon.
That short-haired joy and roughness—
                    America—your stupidity.

I could almost love you again.
We left—onto the freeway shoulders—
                    under the tough old stars—
In the shadow of bluffs
                    I came back to myself,
To the real work, to
                    "What is to be done."

Gary Snyder

Like Gary Snyder, Andy Johnson goes "undercover" into an alien environment, although in this case it is the world of romantic relationships. But where Snyder simply tucks his hair up under his cap and takes out his earring, Andy's speaker employs a deeper, more troubling disguise. Snyder's deception is temporary; it ends as soon as he gets back outside "under the tough old stars." For the speaker in Andy's poem, on the other hand, the deception must continue if he hopes to keep the woman he has deceived under the spell of his "patented half-smile" and "deep brooding stare." Snyder retreats to certainty; Andy remains in uncertainty.

According to Andy, Snyder's poem gave him only a hint of where his own poem would ultimately go. He notes that "I did not get much of a feel for who the narrator was and whether or not this particular bar made him stray very far from his real identity." Nevertheless, "I Went into the Maverick Bar" got Andy wondering: "I sat back and tried to think of when I was most guilty of putting on a mask, and I would say relationships are it for me. My poem made me almost laugh at myself—and then kick myself—when it was done."

In his book *Practical Criticism*, I. A. Richards describes **tone** as the speaker's "attitude towards his listener." In *Writing Poetry*, Barbara Drake modifies that definition to "an expression of the poet's attitude toward the poem's subject." In either case, tone is a quality of the poet's real or adopted **voice**, which M. H. Abrams describes in his *Glossary of Literary Terms* as "the sense of a pervasive presence, a determinate intelligence and moral sensibility, which has selected, ordered, rendered, and expressed these literary materials in just this way." The tone of a poem can be ironic and angry or reverential and solemn, and that tone may or may not reflect the author behind the implied voice.

There are as many subtleties of tone as there are poems and poets to write them. Notice how both Gary Snyder and Andy Johnson manipulate tone in their poems. Snyder adopts the voice of a man who is tolerant enough to see the charm of dancing "like in High School dances / in the fifties," yet too experienced to fully endorse "That short-haired joy and roughness." Instead, he believes that "the real work . . . / [the] What is to be done" must take place outside, under the "tough old stars." Andy wins us over by exposing his own hypocrisy, by revealing the private voice behind the public one. His tone is self-mocking and brutally honest as he discusses the finer points of deceiving a potential lover.

Disguise

My eyebrow curls
And lifts skyward,
The patented half-smile
That yanked you my way.

With an indolent air
And a deep brooding stare,
I'm an insult to the truth.

I'm a million men today:
Rough, tough and expendable.
I float some crap your way
About life being a journey.

To my chagrin, you buy it.
"I'm a free spirit," I lie,
"Just like you."
You smile. I sigh.

Andrew Johnson

Your Turn

Write a poem in which you remember or imagine a time when you put on a disguise and entered a situation that had the potential to be unfriendly, or worse. The disguise may be something as simple as changing your style of dress, or it may be much more elaborate.

As you draft your poem, ask yourself, What is the nature of my narrator's disguise? Is it easy to put on and take off, or does it require a substantial investment of energy? What does my narrator hope to gain by deception? Will the person or people he or she is fooling find out that they have been tricked, or will the disguise never be noticed? Does the narrator believe, like Snyder, that the disguise is necessary and useful, or, like Andy, does he or she feel guilty about wearing a mask?

Chapter Thirty-Five

Fruit

Your poem for this chapter will be about fruit.
While this may at first seem like a rather odd topic
for a poem, it will seem less so if you remember
that most fruits not only taste good, they have a
symbolic value as well. For the ancient Greeks,
grapes evoked Dionysus, the god of sensuality and
fertility. The pomegranate summoned forth the
myth of Demeter and Persephone. For Buddhists,
the banana tree represents the weakness and
instability of the material world. In the Jewish and
Christian religions, apples are associated with
knowledge and sin. Indeed, although apples are
not specifically mentioned, somewhere in both of
the poems in this chapter is the account of Eve's
adventures in the Garden of Eden. That story tells
us that, as sweet as it may taste, stolen fruit, rather
than fruit grown by our own hands, is going to
end up costing a lot more than we expected.

   The speaker in Sylvia Path's "Blackberrying" is
on what ought to be a very pleasant walk,

gathering blackberries as she makes her way to the sea. However, her rather pedestrian adventure seems fraught with unexpected menace. There is "Nobody in the land." The choughs (crowlike birds) are "cacophonous" and look like "Bits of burnt paper wheeling in a blown sky." The wind comes rushing at her, "Slapping its phantom laundry in [her] face." The world has become sinister, and we can see that her sensitivity to its less pleasant aspects will preclude her from ever truly enjoying the fruit she has picked.

Blackberrying

Nobody in the land, and nothing, nothing but blackberries,
Blackberries on either side, though on the right mainly,
A blackberry alley, going down in hooks, and a sea
Somewhere at the end of it, heaving. Blackberries
Big as a the ball of my thumb, and dumb as eyes
Ebon in the hedges, fat
With blue-red juices. These they squander on my fingers.
I had not asked for such a blood sisterhood; they must love
    me.
They accommodate themselves to my milkbottle, flattening
    their sides.

Overhead go the choughs in black, cacophonous flocks—
Bits of burnt paper wheeling in a blown sky.
Theirs is the only voice, protesting, protesting.
I do not think the sea will appear at all.
The high, green meadows are glowing, as if lit from within.
I come to one bush of berries so ripe it is a bush of flies,
Hanging their bluegreen bellies and their wing panes in a
    Chinese screen.
The honey-feast of the berries has stunned them; they
    believe in heaven.
One more hook, and the berries and bushes end.

The only thing to come now is the sea.
From between two hills a sudden wind funnels at me,
Slapping its phantom laundry in my face.
These hills are too green and sweet to have tasted salt.
I follow the sheep path between them. A last hook brings me
To the hills' northern face, and the face is orange rock
That looks out on nothing, nothing but a great space
Of white and pewter lights, and a din like silversmiths
Beating and beating at an intractable metal.

Sylvia Plath

The word *symbol* has been used several times already in this book. As you may already know, a **symbol** is something that represents something else and that inspires a number of additional meanings beyond its literal significance.

In the case of Plath's poem, the act of picking blackberries is undoubtedly symbolic: master poets do not describe the landscape in such vivid terms and with such astounding metaphors simply to prove that they are competent tour guides. Yet symbolic of what, we can only speculate. Blackberries seem to represent something toward which the speaker aspires: they are heavenly, delicious. However, they also have a less desirable aspect. Blackberries are as "dumb as eyes"; their juice is like blood; they attract so many flies that their bushes seem to be "glowing, as if lit from within." For Plath, nothing good is without its bad side, and blackberries are no different. Perhaps they are symbols of something sweet she hopes to obtain—renown in her career as a poet, maybe—and blackberrying is symbolic of a quest that has not been wholly successful. (The sound of the sea making "a din like silversmiths / Beating and beating at an intractable metal" certainly does not seem to bode well.) In any case, though, Plath makes no attempt to show a one-to-one correspondence between blackberrying and whatever else it may represent, nor, most poets and critics would argue, should she.

While a poet may decide beforehand that she is going to use a particular object or person in her poem, chances are the most evocative images will occur to the writer in the process of composition rather than as a result of painstaking forethought. Moreover, the most interesting symbols may, like Plath's blackberries, have myriad and enigmatic meanings. In a word, it is probably better to let your symbols come to you than to assiduously seek them out. The result of too much deliberate symbol making can be heavy-handed and silly.

Frank Avery's choice of a symbolic fruit is similar to Plath's, but where her poem finishes on a note of despair, Frank ends his in defiance. "The Raspberries Next Door" focuses on a memory from the speaker's childhood that left him shaken and changed. While snitching raspberries from his fussy, childless neighbors, Frank is accosted and yelled at. The experience of seeing adults act as out of control as children is a new and shocking one, but it leaves him feeling strangely bold. Unlike Plath, he is still able to enjoy his stolen fruit, despite the verbal punishment he receives. For Frank, "the taste was tart, yet sweet / because forbidden."

The Raspberries Next Door

When I was six, we lived next door
to the Slades. Planted against
their garage, no windows in sight,
was a raspberry bush that would come
to life in summer. The Slades
were childless, and they didn't like us
three Avery kids one bit.
We were always whapping

their windows with wiffle balls
and jumping their fence
to retrieve a stray Nerf.

One day Mrs. Slade caught me
plucking berries. She grabbed
my skinny arm and screamed
until her husband ran outside.
Then they both stood there
yelling at me, in a rage
I didn't think grown-ups
were capable of. I trembled,
but I felt defiant, too.
The last raspberry was still
on my tongue, the skin slightly hairy,
the seeds were half-crunched
between my teeth. And the taste—
the taste was tart, yet sweet
because forbidden.

Frank Avery

Your Turn

Fruit may sound like a less than promising focus for a poem, but it is really not that uncommon a topic. What, for instance, would John Milton's *Paradise Lost* or John Keats's "To Autumn" or Robert Frost's "After Apple-Picking" be without apples? Indeed, one of the great middle-length poems in English, Christina Rossetti's "Goblin Market," includes a number of rapturous descriptions of young women eating fruit.

Write a poem that features fruit in some important way. To avoid bland generalizations, you should probably name and focus on just one or two types of fruit. Ideally, you will have the fruit in front of you as you write, although if that is impossible, at the very least have a picture you can look at to help animate your memory and arouse your taste buds.

Chapter Thirty-Six

Insects

"The Brown Menace" was published in 1973, a time of heightened political activism, by Audre Lorde, a poet deeply committed to the improvement of the lives of African Americans. As even a cursory reading will reveal, the poem is not just about roaches. Yet Lorde uses an essential quality of these insects—their indestructibility— to comment on the relations between people of color and the dominant culture. Your poem, too, should use a species of insect to make a statement about the human world.

The relationship between humans and roaches is an odd one, and Lorde exploits this peculiarity. We detest roaches because they carry diseases, because they represent uncleanliness and poverty. We go to great lengths—using sprays and powders that may even be harmful to us—in an attempt to wipe the loathsome creatures out. Cockroaches frighten us: they are, as Lorde writes, the "nightmare on your white pillow."

Nevertheless, we also admire their ability to survive. We have all heard that if there is a nuclear war, cockroaches will be among the few creatures left alive. Lorde draws a parallel between humans' reaction to roaches and the response of Caucasians toward African Americans. If whites are afraid of blacks, they also "learn to honor . . . / by imitation." Speaking both from her imaginary vantage as an insect, and from her real stance as an African American woman, Lorde writes "Call me / your own determination / in the most detestable shape." Her implication is that her adversarial audience has more in common with "the brown menace" than it cares to admit.

The Brown Menace Or Poem To The Survival Of Roaches

Call me
your deepest urge
toward survival
call me
and my brothers and sisters
in the sharp smell of your refusal
call me
roach and presumptuous
nightmare on your white pillow
your itch to destroy
the indestructible
part of yourself.

Call me
your own determination
in the most detestable shape
you can become
friend of your own image
within me
I am you
in your most deeply cherished nightmare
scuttling through the painted cracks
you create to admit me
into your kitchens into your fearful midnights
into your values at noon
in your most secret places
with hate
you learn to honor me
by imitation
as I alter—
through your greedy preoccupations

through your kitchen wars
through your poisonous refusal—

To survive.
To survive.

Audre Lorde

Whatever else "The Brown Menace Or Poem To The Survival Of Roaches" is, it is also an example of **political poetry:** it seeks to change or confirm the reader's opinion on a public matter, in this case, race relations. Critic Jerome Brooks has noted that "Lorde is a poet for whom writing is a serious moral responsibility." Granted, this is a description that could apply to any number of poets, but for writers like Lorde, who believe we are bound by political restraints and obligations, moral responsibility is at the heart of why they write in the first place.

Political poetry has a long history in world literature, from the epic oral poetry of African cultures and the politically charged lyrics of early Greeks like Solon to twentieth-century figures like the Nobel Prize-winning Bengali poet Rabindranath Tagore and South American statesman-writer Pablo Neruda. In America, however, political poetry has often been regarded with suspicion. Many literary critics have insisted that poetry that has political persuasion as its primary aim becomes less successful *as poetry* and sounds, instead, more like the sort of partisan harangue one tends to find in political pamphlets.

This is not an issue that will ever be conclusively settled. You may sympathize with those writers who feel unqualified to make the larger statements political poetry seems to require. Still, if you find your poetry is mostly about yourself and the people you know well, you might consider taking a broader view of America just to see where it leads.

Kelly Janssen transfers the focus of her poem from the public to the private realm. In a meditation that apparently takes place after the fact, the narrator describes Matt, a sinister former boyfriend. What the narrator sees in this repulsive young man is difficult to know; apparently, one of his favorite pastimes is plucking the legs from daddy longlegs spiders. We may also wonder why the speaker dwells on this particular behavior—until the last line reveals the significance of the insect-human connection.

Daddy
Longlegs

Only two months behind me,
And only one cornfield away,
My boyfriend Matt, seventeen
And weird as hell, loved
To master the fate of daddy
Longlegs. Every time
An innocent victim ambled
Onto his shoe, he laughed
Wickedly and picked up

The unsuspecting spider.
One by one, he'd pluck
The legs off, placing
The dismembered body
On the ground, watching
It attempt to lumber away.
Like tweezing eyebrows,
He pulled those "hairs" out
Until all that remained
Was the body, raisin-like,
Which couldn't move at all.
Then he'd shrug his scrawny
Shoulders and kiss me goodbye.

I hated being that daddy longlegs.

Kelly Janssen

Your Turn

Choose a species of insect and use one or more of its key characteristics to comment on the human world. Be inventive. Try to avoid obvious and well-worn examples: people are all ants or bees mindlessly dashing around, or a lover is like a moth drawn to a flame. The odder the creature you choose, the more inventive your poem will have to be.

Consider researching and writing about one of the unusual insects from the following list: assassin bug, boll weevil, buffalo bug, cone-nose, dung beetle, earwig, glowworm, kissing bug, mealworm, punkie, robber fly, silverfish, stinkbug, tsetse fly, or weevil.

Chapter Thirty-Seven

An Eminent Conversation

If you have ever wondered what it would be like if two historical figures you admire (or despise) had the opportunity to talk with each other, the subject of this chapter's poems should be intriguing. Your assignment is to write a dialogue between two famous people.

In Amiri Baraka's model poem, "Buddha Asked Monk," the exchange between the Buddha and jazz pianist Thelonius Monk is appropriately brief, with Monk giving a Zen-like response to the Buddha's *koan* (a **koan** is a riddle in the form of a parable). The genius of this tiny poem is that, despite its brevity, we can meditate on it for quite a while.

It is odd, for one thing, that the famous Eastern sage is asking a question of a contemporary American musician. Does the Buddha's question imply that he thinks *he* is always right, or is the Buddha recognizing that everything Monk does is correct? (The pun lurking in the title seems to suggest that the pianist is as wise as a Buddhist monk.) And what are we to make of Thelonius Monk's response? If you have read Buddhist koans before, you probably hear a note of chastisement in Monk's answer: *If you have to ask, you'll never know* (as Louis Armstrong was supposed to have said when asked to define jazz).

Yet the "Blue and / Invisible" Monk—whose life, like anyone's, was full of mistakes and hard times—may have no more of an answer to the Buddha's question than we do. No matter how you interpret the poem, there can be no doubt that it is made more evocative because its two speakers are famous: just replace "Buddha" and "Monk" with "Nancy" and "Bob" to see how much is lost.

Buddha Asked Monk

"If you were always right
Would it be Easier
or more Difficult
Living in The World?"

"I knew you'd ask that!"
Monk said, Blue and
Invisible.

Amiri Baraka

"Buddha Asked Monk" alludes to Eastern religion and the hard bop jazz of the 1940s and 1950s. Jamie Molitor's poem takes the form of an extended dialogue between two speakers who are probably more familiar to American students: Jim Morrison of The Doors and Edgar Allan Poe. This turns out to be a very appropriate pairing, for both men had similar visions of the world, both were obsessed with love and death, and both have become cultural heroes. Jamie's clever allusions to Morrison and Poe's work increases our delight in the poem. (An **allusion** is a reference to a person, place, thing, event, or idea outside the work itself.) Moreover, Jamie's use of the ballad stanza is just the right choice to tell the story of two storytelling poets.

One of the oldest poetic forms in English is the **ballad.** Ballads are composed of **ballad stanzas,** each of which is four lines long. The lines alternate between iambic tetrameter (four stressed syllables per line) and iambic trimeter (three stressed syllables per line), with the final words rhyming *abcb.* Among the famous ballads you may have read in introductory literature courses are "Sir Patrick Spens," "Lord Randal," and "The Demon Lover."

Aside from these technical considerations, ballads have several other common characteristics. J. A. Cuddon notes five of these traits, four of which can be found in Jamie's poem: "a) the beginning is often abrupt; b) the language is simple; c) the story is told through dialogue and action; d) the theme is often tragic (though there are a number of comic ballads); (e) there is often a refrain." While Jamie's poem does not have a refrain, the other characteristics of a ballad are present. Incidentally, this is not, as Jamie admits, because he has made a thorough study of the form, but rather because he has internalized these qualities from his reading in literature classes and from his knowledge of the ballad's present-day heir, the popular song.

The Lizard King and Poe

A Spanish caravan entered the fields
    led by the Lizard King.
He saw up ahead the profile of Poe;
    a silent, motionless thing.

Poe gazed through the dark and wretched storm
    at the riders making their way.
Then noticed the raven perched by his side
    in an old snag, withered and gray.

He asked his companion, "What could they want,
    from a simple man like me?"
"Perhaps they're coming to take me away
    for my dealings with Annabel Lee."

The King stopped his steed with whiskey in hand
    and took down a shot or two.
And Poe took a sip from his laudanum flask—
    feeling it overdue.

"Good day to you, Sir," said the poet of old
    as he wiped the drip from his chin.
"What business have you in Elysian Fields
    which you are riding in?"

"We've lost our way to the Whiskey Bar,"
    he whispered in Poe's ear.
"We're in search of spirits far different from those
    we seem to be finding here.

"Perhaps you could show me the quickest way
    to break through to the other side?
We've traveled so long, our bodies are sore,
    and we wish no more to ride."

And then Poe's reply came quick and cold
    with a wrinkle in his brow.
"These fields are harsh and the people are strange,
    but I must tell you now . . .

"Your ballroom days are over, Son.
    You couldn't break through if you tried.
Jim, you, most of all, should know:
    No one here gets out alive."

Jamie Molitor

Your Turn

Write a poem that takes the form of a dialogue between two famous people. The two can be dead or alive, and they do not have to have lived at the same time. Try to think of two individuals who are not normally paired but who still might have interesting things to say to each other. Jesus talking with St. Paul, for instance, would not be as suggestive as Jesus talking with Hitler.

A few examples of interesting (and sometimes outrageous) pairings generated by one group of students included the following: Joseph Stalin and Queen Elizabeth, Sigmund Freud and Dr. Ruth, Christopher Columbus and Frederick Douglass, Kurt Cobain and Charles Darwin, and Albert Einstein and Ice Cube.

Chapter Thirty-Eight

Suppose

One of the pastimes children enjoy most is playing make-believe. They love to imagine that they are someone or something other than who they really are. Writers, no matter their age, also enjoy pretending, and your assignment for this chapter is to write a poem in which you transform a person or thing into something entirely different.

Pattiann Rogers plays a very sophisticated form of this particular game in "Suppose Your Father Was a Redbird." Not only does she ask us to picture our fathers and ourselves as redbirds, she tells us very precisely what that experience would be like.

Rogers, who is well-known for the scientific accuracy of her poems, employs a wealth of factual details to help the reader envision the bizarre transmutation she suggests. Notice how much information she conveys in just the first stanza. A lesser poet might have said something like "he had pretty red wings." Rogers, though, gives us "the meticulous layering / Of graduated down." She tells us that the rows of feathers increase in size until they reach "the hard-splayed / Wine-gloss tips." Despite the fact that, until you read this poem, you have probably never in your life imagined your father as a redbird, now you can.

Suppose Your Father Was a Redbird

Suppose his body was the meticulous layering
Of graduated down which you studied early,
Rows of feathers increasing in size to the hard-splayed
Wine-gloss tips of his outer edges.

Suppose, before you could speak, you watched
The slow spread of his wing over and over,
The appearance of that invisible appendage,
The unfolding transformation of his body to the airborne.
And you followed his departure again and again,
Learning to distinguish the red microbe of his being
Far into the line of the horizon.

Then today you might be the only one able to see
The breast of a single red bloom
Five miles away across an open field.
The modification of your eye might have enabled you
To spot a red moth hanging on an oak branch
In the exact center of the Aurorean Forest.
And you could define for us, "hearing red in the air,"
As you predict the day pollen from the poppy
Will blow in from the valley.

Naturally you would picture your faith arranged
In filamented principles moving from pink
To crimson at the final quill. And the red tremble
Of your dream you might explain as the shimmer
Of his back lost over the sea at dawn.
Your sudden visions you might interpret as the uncrossing
Of heaven, the bones of the sky spread,
The conceptualized wing of the mind untangling.

Imagine the intensity of your revelation
The night the entire body of a star turns red
And you watch it as it rushes in flames
Across the black, down into the hills.

If your father was a redbird,
Then you would be obligated to try to understand
What it is you recognize in the sun
As you study it again this evening
Pulling itself and the sky in dark red
Over the edge of the earth.

Pattiann Rogers

Too often we tend to separate the sciences from the humanities, as though they had absolutely nothing in common. Granted, an overly creative approach to a subject like mathematics, one that ignored the accepted properties of numbers, would not find favor with many mathematicians. Likewise, a mathematician who wrote "poems" using only axioms and postulates would probably not go far in the poetry world.

Nevertheless, scientists do draw on the humanities, especially literature. They frequently use metaphors and similes to explain complicated abstract problems. They borrow figures from Greek and Roman mythology when they name new creatures or phenomena. Physicist Murray Gell-Mann updated this tradition when he named one of the hypothetical elementary particles "quark" after a line in James Joyce's *Finnegan's Wake.*

In return, poets like Pattiann Rogers have demonstrated that there is plenty of poetic material to be found in the scientific arena. These writers believe that, far from bogging them down in the prosaic real world, subjects like physics, biology, genetics, chemistry, astronomy, and geology are all gateways to fascinating new poems.

While Rogers's poem is philosophical and fastidious in its descriptions, Kristi Yurs takes a decidedly lighter approach in "Suppose My Dog Was an Angelfish." She hasn't consulted a zoologist about either dogs or tropical fish. Still, she knows enough about the latter to give them specific names—"blue damsels, wrasses, / and bright yellow tangs." Moreover, her close observation of her dog's playful behavior enables Kristi to envision the dog diving in and out of a toy treasure chest and swimming "circles / around all the other fish."

Suppose
My Dog
Was an
Angelfish

Suppose she lived
in a 55 gallon saltwater tank
with blue damsels, wrasses,
and bright yellow tangs.
Instead of playing
with her favorite stuffed animal,
she could dive in and out
of a golden treasure chest.
Imagine her narrow body
maneuvering past the rocks,

her long pointed tail
peeking through fan coral.
Her neon colors
would light up the water
as she swam circles
around all the other fish.

Kristi Yurs

Your Turn

Write a poem in which you imagine that someone or something (like your father or your dog) has become something (like a redbird or an angelfish) other than what it really is. You may benefit from research here. If, for instance, you want the reader to suppose that your friend is a piece of quartz, it will be useful to know that quartz is the second most common of all minerals; that it is found in igneous, metamorphic, and sedimentary rocks; that it is sometimes transparent, other times translucent; that it has a number of industrial uses; that in certain situations it can produce electric voltage; and that it sometimes contains precious metals such as gold.

What you do with these facts is, of course, limited only by your imagination. You might use your knowledge of quartz's ability to produce electricity to suggest how electric your friend is in a specific circumstance. Or you could indicate her hidden value by alluding to the gold in a vein of quartz. In any case, there should be at least several significant correlations between your original subject and the thing into which you transform it.

Chapter Thirty-Nine

Pets

While many of the assignments in this book can be completed without confronting any especially uncomfortable emotions, others necessarily require you to face less pleasant aspects of the world. Poetry, after all, must address sorrow as well as sweetness, and in Chapter Thirty-Nine you are asked to write a poem about the death of a pet.

Anyone who has ever had a pet knows that the ties we have to our domesticated animals are sometimes as strong as those we have with people, if not stronger. Unfortunately, when we write about the deaths of pets, we tend to become excessively sentimental, and many creative writing instructors make the deaths of pets one of the few off-limits subjects for poems. These teachers may never have seen a good poem on that topic and probably do not believe one is possible.

Billy Collins's "Putting Down the Cat" is exceptional in that it manages to convey powerful emotions without becoming lachrymose. Collins performs this exacting feat by avoiding the obvious memories—his cat purring contentedly in the sunlight, say, or playfully batting around a toy mouse—and focusing instead on a single significant moment in the present: the veterinarian's fatal injection. In fact, what is so touching about this poem is that the speaker refuses to ascribe human qualities to his cat, who "cannot count at all, / much less to a hundred, much less backwards."

Putting Down the Cat

The assistant holds her on the table,
the fur hanging limp from her tiny skeleton,
and the veterinarian raises the needle of fluid
which will put the line through her ninth life.

"Painless," he reassures me, "like counting
backwards from a hundred," but I want to tell him
that our poor cat cannot count at all,
much less to a hundred, much less backwards.

Billy Collins

Throughout this book, I warn against excessive **sentimentality.** In his *Glossary of Literary Terms,* M. H. Abrams defines *sentimentalism* as "a pejorative term applied to what is perceived as an excess of emotion to an occasion, or, in a more limited sense, to an overindulgence in the 'tender' emotions of pathos and sympathy." Clearly, these are the very sorts of emotions that are likely to be evoked by the death of a pet.

Billy Collins and Pam Dwyer, the student poet following Collins's example, refuse to "overindulge" in pity and sympathy for the passing of their pets. Both authors implicitly acknowledge and observe the limits society places on how much we ought to mourn. In our culture it is acceptable for a mother who has lost her son to grieve visibly, perhaps to refuse food for a while or to take several weeks off work. Yet such a reaction to the death of a goldfish would be considered "an excess of emotion to [the] occasion."

The most likely reason that so many beginning writers feel it is okay for poetry to be sentimental is that the most popular, widespread form of poetry is often *very* sappy indeed. Greeting cards, which can be purchased in any supermarket or drugstore, thrive on mushy emotions. (In fact, "get well," anniversary, and birthday cards are so notoriously sentimental that alternative lines of sarcastic cards are now a staple of the industry.) But a literary poem, it is important to remember, is *not* a greeting card. If you want your work to be taken seriously, you must be aware of the line between poetry and schmaltz.

Pam Dwyer's poem is about a subject that, cynics might say, is even less worthy of poetic attention than a cat: her hamster, Simon. Yet for Pam, who was ten at the time, the death of Simon initially made her feel as though "the world would end, / the sun would never rise again." The use of clichés in the first stanza seems intentional, for Pam is honest about the depth of her sorrow. The passage of just a single day makes her forget about Simon and the next morning "the sun was there, / tiny, gray and cold / in the winter sky."

Simon

The morning Simon died
I thought the world would end,
the sun would never rise again.
He was curled up like a fetus.
His fur was sticky wet.

"It's just a stupid hamster,"
my brother taunted.
Dad told me, "Okay. Enough
foolishness. Wipe your tears
and make sure you've got
your math homework."

It was February. All day,
I sat at my desk, staring
at the pictures of George Washington Carver
and Martin Luther King.

Fifth grade seemed like a torture
especially designed
for sensitive people like me.

I thought about Simon:
Was there a heaven for hamsters?
Would God greet him at the gate,
or send a little furry angel instead?

That night after dinner I watched TV,
forgot all about Simon
until the next morning
when I looked out my window:

the sun was there,
tiny, gray and cold
in the winter sky.

Pam Dwyer

Your Turn

Write a poem about the death of a pet. Whether you draw on your own experience or simply imagine the event, concentrate on using specific details and avoiding clichés. Unlike the elegy for a person, the elegy for a pet cannot sustain high-flown language for very long.

The following question set may trigger a memory that helps you write your poem: What was your pet's most unusual characteristic or its most annoying one? Did the pet belong only to you or to other family members? How did they react to its death? How did the pet die? Was its death the result of circumstances outside your control or, like Collins, did you have a hand in what happened?

Chapter Forty

Rearranging Memory

Holy *cow!* you may say after reading "When one travels, one might 'hit' a storm," *what was that?* Lyn Hejinian's poem is certainly one of the more difficult models in this book. That difficulty stems in large part from the fact that Hejinian's mission as a writer is radically different from that of most of the other poets you have read so far. Rather than seeking to bring her poems to closure, which she believes ignores the ambiguity and incompleteness of our daily lives, Hejinian argues for "the fundamental necessity of openness" in poetry.

Nevertheless, she, like many other experimental poets, is attracted to forms that can help channel the often turbulent stream of words that comes flowing out when she writes. According to Hejinian's publisher, Sun and Moon Press, "Writing it in her 37th year, Hejinian constructed a work of 37 sections of 37 sentences, each section paralleling the year of her life." The second edition, from which this excerpt is taken, "added 8 sections and 8 new sentences to each previous section to account for her current age." The selection below, "When one travels, one might 'hit' a storm," corresponds to the eighteenth year of Hejinian's life. Therefore, the poem is composed of 45 sentences that loosely and impressionistically "describe" the poet's first year at college, a time when she was encountering interesting new ideas ("the choral director described the torso in terms of the muscles of sound") yet still had to take P.E., a time when she was both hesitant to make waves ("I was reluctant to be disconcerting, to cause discontinuity") but also full of questions about her own beliefs ("Religion is a vague lowing"). Your poem, too, should consist of the same number of sentences as your current age and focus on a single year of your life.

Hejinian has sometimes been called a Language poet. **Language poetry** is an experimental movement that emerged in the 1970s and values playful irony, fragmentation, subjectivity, and "open" forms. Like Jackson Pollack, who created memorable paintings by splattering paint across huge canvases, language poets have expressed an interest in scattering words, phrases, and sentences on the page, believing that the unexpected juxtapositions they create reveal more about life at the end of our chaotic century than more traditional poems.

When one travels, one might "hit" a storm

It flies in the night. In that light it is obvious that you are related to your mother. Boots, plows, cheese, burls. As for we who "love to be astonished," the night is lit. Remarkably to learn to look. My father would say I've a "big day" tomorrow. Words are not always adequate to the occasion, and my "probably" sounded hopeless. It's real, why, so it's wrong. I mentioned my face because I am made that way wonderfully like a shadow I do not despise. But if I don't like the first dress I try on, I will not like any. It is only a coincidence. Whose shadows who's. At the circus the elephants were more beautiful than the horses, more touching than the clowns, and more graceful than the tigers trained to jump on their backs. Physical education was required. At school, the choral director described the torso in terms of the muscles of sound. Always infinity extends from any individual life, but eternity is limited between one's birth and one's death. Interpreting such combinations of events, and the sort of mysticism on which such interpretations are based, is what gives coincidence its bad name. Religion is a vague lowing. I was beginning to look for some meaning when I should have been satisfied with events. It is hard to run away from moving water. For the time, being; twilight seen even full. I mean to say "hopelessly" in a promising tone, as one would say, "hopelessly in love," and mean, really, "very much," and, especially, "full of hope." In my "trouble with conflict," I was reluctant to be disconcerting, to cause discontinuity. Panic versus crystallographic form. Knickknacks are for browsers. There is some discomfort more active than boredom but none more fatiguing. I had gone back to bed and was pretending to sleep in order to avoid saying goodbye to the friends who had been visiting, hiding from farewell's display. The lives of which I read seemed more real than my own, but I still seemed more real than the persons who had led them. A sunlit winter's day lay thin, frozen to the hummocks and rubble of mud in the cold but erotic marshlands beside the Concord River. We have come a long way from what we actually felt. But he remains aloof, saying only that things *seem* familiar. The invisible but realistic detail of an ultimate monument. By hand, put together, with hood and thread. Poco Bueno was buried, saddled, standing. To do things for the sake of fame or other gain is selfish, but to do them for your own pleasure is to do them generously. One might become a volunteer down with the poor Italians. At least, we shall solve the riddle presented by money, or so he says. It seemed that we had hardly begun and we were already there. Memory is the money of my class. What a vast! what a business! The lowly cabbage strives and the turnip in the garden yearns to be a person. You know, things like that. Systems betray, or are, as in a "made place," made betrayals. I was organized by addition and addiction. I found a penny in a calla lily.

Lyn Hejinian

As critic Paul Hoover notes, language poets favor the **prose poem,** a short piece of writing that has no line breaks or regular rhythmic pattern but that still has some of the qualities of poetry, such as compact and imagistic language. Hoover praises the prose poem for "its formal freedom and exhaustiveness," and goes on to say that "the language poet builds up a mosaic structure by means of seemingly unrelated sentences and sentence fragments. The progression of non sequiturs frustrates the reader's expectation of linear development at the same time that it opens a more complete world of reference. The emphasis in language poetry is placed on *production* rather than *packaging* (beginning, middle, end) and ease of consumption."

There are both advantages and drawbacks to writing poetry in prose, especially experimental poetry. On the positive side, you don't have to worry about enjambment or how the poem "looks" on the page (it will look like a paragraph of prose). On the other hand, helpful technical aids like meter, rhyme, and so forth are not available to the prose poet, who must also be careful not to drift into the less intense rhythms of most expository prose. Still, the form possesses a hybrid's adaptability to subject and tone, capable of ranging—to name a few twentieth century American examples—from Russell Edson's exhilarating silliness to W. S. Merwin's haunting somberness. As David Young, editor of an anthology of prose poetry, writes, "The prose poem is a very special invention, like a chair that flies or a small dish that produces food for forty people."

Because this is one of the trickier assignments in the book, two student examples are given below. Although both student poets initially found Hejinian's example daunting, they discovered that once they put aside their habit of making connections from one sentence to the next and "just wrote," the sentences came tumbling out. Sarah and Heather found that they had to approach the poem counterintuitively. Years of training in English courses taught them to be logical. They resisted. And so, like "maps of a mind," to steal Sarah's title, these two prose poems summon us into the authors' memories of their earlier lives.

Map of a Mind

Welcome to New Jersey. I never knew what it was to fish in Chesapeake Bay. Red carpet down, around and around. From the castle turret is visible the store with the orange sign where blood poured from a three year old's head. The last time I saw the schnitzel lady in the little white booth, she smiled at me. When you realize this is not the same place, just the same people. An invitation to fifteen years of long-distance friendship. Man changed time and children walked to school in daylight. An entity of solely yourself, and the apple seed of responsibility toward all others. I realized I would never trick or treat in snow again and I cried. The stone said Susan, she was our mother's too. No, he is not my brother . . . but I wish he were. Tchaikovsky, a Ouija board, and The Best Little Girl in the World. Death Be Not Proud, but try and some will succeed. Green and white, green and white, Alice ate the cake and shrank. This is the end and the beginning again as salad cries for dressing. I want to disappear from you and hide behind a slim, young birch. Life is blood red, staining our faces in a rush of relieved good-byes. Candy corn is hyper, happy sugar high at midnight. Wrap yourself in a blue flannel sheet like I Never Promised You a Rose Garden. If my feet are on earth and I have the moon in my hands, may I declare victory, or must I keep on trudging?

Sarah Brown

Maricopa County

The wind at my face. Bikes, kites, riding on the hood of a slow-moving car. Spear a cactus with a pencil, the juice drips, dries, heals the wound. The day of womanhood. Backsides of barns, moss-rooted, adorned with peacocks. Overdue fines at the Glendale Public library. I was the young confidently unconfident female feigning to fit with big brother's friends. Oh, Johnny. Moonlit walks left me lying on the warm concrete wondering where the stars were. Coke nails in typing class, clip 'em, clip 'em. "Impale," she shoves the pencil through the paper, violently. Les Miserables, Victor Hugo, Toothless Fantene. Walton reruns in early morning mist as I walk the booming lady with her caddie next door. Roses never grew. Quarters unlimited for babysitting laundry. Crystal Caverns. Squad cars, dogs snooping under the pine. "How was I supposed to know it was the Mayor's house?" Reeses Peanut Butter Cups, Dads Root Beer, Cemetery Picnics. He hit me in the face, hee hee hee. Waiting for the dark, pop the screen, escape undetected—ooo power. Sunday morning naps at Faith Bible Church. Rhett, the motorcycle man, who would whisk me away to prom. Paige turned page after page, speechlessly ignoring me.

Heather Cramer

Your Turn

Follow Hejinian's lead and write an autobiographical prose poem that consists of the same number of sentences as your current age. If, for instance, you are 19 and you want to write about your life at age 5, your poem will consist of 19 sentences focusing on what you remember of yourself as a kindergartner. Remember that this is a *prose* poem. Do *not* break your sentences at the right margin, but instead allow them to wrap around the way they would if you were writing a story or an essay.

Like Hejinian, you should move from memory to memory without explaining your connections. In fact, it will be useful to avoid transitions altogether. Instead, zero in on brief moments that, when juxtaposed against other memories, give the reader a suggestion, not an explanation, of your emotional life at the time. Your natural inclination when writing this poem will be to connect things up, to link, to make sense. For the duration of this assignment, try to withstand these urges.

Chapter Forty-One

Envisioning One's Audience

The question of audience is one all writers must eventually address. On one end of the spectrum are those who write only for themselves. These people keep a diary or journal but never show it to anyone. At the opposite extreme are people who measure their success solely in "units sold." Most of us fall somewhere in the middle. Writing is an important activity in our lives, one we value in and of itself. We *do,* however, want at least a few people to read what we have written once we are done. The poem you draft for this chapter will focus on the question of audience: Who do you envision as your primary readership?

Gerald Locklin's poem makes clear what you may have already suspected: the audience for poetry is composed of a number of different "constituencies." According to the speaker's friend,

Lara, in order to be successful, it is important for a poet to identify and relate closely to his or her audience. Lara mentions several of the poets in this book—Denise Levertov, Amiri Baraka, and Gary Soto—as writers with a loyal fan base. Unfortunately, the problem (as she sees it) is that the members of Locklin's constituency "either don't or can't read at all." Clearly, this remark is humorous, but it does point to a more serious matter: to whom does the poet of the poorly read and the illiterate address his poetry? For Gerald Locklin, whom Charles Bukowski called "one of the great undiscovered talents of our time," the issue remains problematic.

a constituency of dunces

"you know," lara says,
"adrienne rich can always count on
five hundred feminists showing up
for her readings.

and amiri baraka and ishmael reed
can count on the blacks
and politically involved readers
will flock to hear carolyn forché,

and bob and dennis draw the gays
and gary soto the chicanos.
and ferlinghetti and levertov
have fame and politics both:

i mean, it's not that these writers can't write—
i just mean that they also have their followings
that they can count on."

"where's mine?" I ask.

"your problem," she says, "is that the people
to whom your work might appeal
do not read poetry.
in fact, most of those
who might share your attitudes or viewpoint

either don't or can't read at all."

Gerald Locklin

Sooner or later, most poets read their poetry aloud. Whether it is at a coffee house or a friend's house, a public library or a pub, chances are that someday you will find yourself on stage having to perform. In fact, so popular have poetry readings become—in part because of the hard work of poet-impresarios like Marc Smith—that an entire subculture has evolved that values oral poetry more than written work. **Slam** or **performance poets** typically memorize their work and employ a well-rehearsed delivery, sometimes incorporating actors' gestures, even stage props, into their presentations.

Gerald Locklin is a literature professor, and he clearly appreciates *written* poetry as much as "spokenword" (another common label for performance poetry). Still, Locklin's work is featured in anthologies like *Stand-Up Poetry,* and he is, indeed, an outstanding reader of his own work. At any rate, a poem such as "a constituency of dunces" has an obviously performative aspect. It is a dialogue between two people, and we are used to seeing dialogues on stage. The language is straightforward and would be easy to understand even if you were sitting in a crowded, noisy audience. (Incidentally, poems that attempt to explain the mystery of life generally tend to flop in performance, unless your audience is very patient or composed mostly of close relatives.) Finally, the last line constitutes a kind of punch line for the rest of the poem.

Katy Montgomery has no such worries about her own imagined audience. Unlike the rather unruly and uneducated crowd Locklin expects to draw, Katy's ideal constituency is composed of people who appreciate "decipherable vocabulary / and grammatical phrases," who still cherish their childhood books. Turned off by some of the more negative poetry that was written by her classmates, Katy was glad to be able to envision a less pessimistic group of readers, "Peter Pan soulmates" who would share her love of innocence and good cheer.

One More
Trip to
Nevernever
Land

I'm sure if I ever collected
my poems into an anthology
I'd have to call it something like
One More Trip to Nevernever Land.
That way everyone who's looking for
bitter truths and harsh realities, anger,
cuss words, and sexual allusions
would know not to buy it.

Maybe I'd add a clause to that title:
"In Plain English." Then
the intellectual types couldn't
be too disappointed over
my decipherable vocabulary
and grammatical phrases.

For those who love details, however,
those who can tell from the streak
of dirt on a Lost Boy's faded

cut-off shorts that he really is lost,
and those who think of childhood
when they "think of a wonderful thought,"
for all my Peter Pan soulmates,
this book would be for you.

Katy Montgomery

Your Turn

While a very few of us may insist that we write *only* for ourselves, if you are reading this book, you probably hope to have at least some kind of an audience. In their humorous, self-deprecating poems, Gerald Locklin and Katy Montgomery envision the sort of people who are likely to enjoy their work.

Write a poem in which you, too, imagine the audience to which your poetry is most likely to appeal. Is your constituency composed mostly of friends and family, or are they primarily strangers? Do they demand a certain type of writing from you, or do they encourage you to experiment? Do you anticipate that your audience will expand over time? If so, who will it include in the future that it doesn't include now? Finally, you might ask yourself if there is a particular group that is inclined to actively *dislike* your work? If there is, how do you respond to that aversion?

Chapter Forty-Two

Beginnings

Most of us are curious about how our parents got together. Were they a well- or ill-matched couple? What sort of misconceptions did they have about each other? Did the circumstances of their union bode well for our future, or was this an event that should never have taken place? Your assignment for this chapter is to address questions like these, as you write a poem that describes the events leading to your birth.

Sharon Olds, writing in her typically frank, uncompromising manner, has few illusions about her mother and father's compatibility as mates and suitability as parents. Although "they are / innocent, they would never hurt anybody," they are simply not cut out for the lives they are about to lead.

Olds envisions what she would tell them if she could go back in time: "you are going to do bad things to children, / you are going to suffer in ways you never heard of, / you are going to want

185

to die." Yet she knows that if she were able to show them the future, she would never exist, so—despite all the pain that will ensue—she "allows" the union to go forth. "Do what you are going to do," she says, her voice both resigned and defiant, "and I will tell about it."

I Go Back to May 1937

I see them standing at the formal gates of their colleges,
I see my father strolling out
under the ochre sandstone arch, the
red tiles glinting like bent
plates of blood behind his head, I
see my mother with a few light books at her hip
standing at the pillar made of tiny bricks with the
wrought-iron gate still open behind her, its
sword-tips black in the May air,
they are about to graduate, they are about to get married,
they are kids, they are dumb, all they know is they are
innocent, they would never hurt anybody.
I want to go up to them and say Stop,
don't do it—she's the wrong woman,
he's the wrong man, you are going to do things
you cannot imagine you would ever do,
you are going to do bad things to children,
you are going to suffer in ways you never heard of,
you are going to want to die. I want to go
up to them there in the late May sunlight and say it,
her hungry pretty blank face turning to me,
her pitiful beautiful untouched body,
his arrogant handsome blind face turning to me,
his pitiful beautiful untouched body,
but I don't do it. I want to live. I
take them up like male and female
paper dolls and bang them together
at the hips like chips of flint as if to
strike sparks from them, I say
Do what you are going to do, and I will tell about it.

Sharon Olds

Most of "I Go Back to May 1937" is set at the end of the academic year, before the narrator's parents were married. Her mother's face is "blank"; her father's is "blind." The connection between the two people is still undeveloped. In contrast, Anna Elkins's poem "Beginning on *The Carla Sea*, February 1976" sets the scene much later in her own parents' relationship: on the night of her conception.

While Anna's poem is clearly a variation on Olds's theme, the younger poet's take on her beginnings is tender rather than angry. The scenario she sketches is one of luxury and ease: "Dad picking at buttered lobster and / Mom sipping a pink drink toward St. Thomas." And the maturity level of the two prospective parents is much higher: "they have been married four years, / have waited and saved to lean against / these starboard rails."

But it is not just the dissimilarity of tone and emotional attachment that differentiates these two poems. Even the season and time of day are very unlike. Where Olds's poem takes place in May sunlight, which seems to expose her parents' faults and prompt them into springtime foolishness, Anna's poem is set at night in the Caribbean in February. The ship cruising the warm seas provides a respite from the harsher climate from which the young couple have presumably escaped. In short, Anna's poem is just as meditative as the model poem, but she has taken the occasion suggested by that piece and moved in an entirely different direction.

Beginning on *The Carla Sea,* February 1976

I watch them standing by ice swans melting
onto starfruit and pomegranates—
Dad picking at buttered lobster and
Mom sipping a pink drink toward St. Thomas.
Later, they wander on deck, past white and red
life preservers and thick braids of brown rope.
Mom's new cotton dress blows against her shiny shins,
Dad keeps close, his thick-hemmed shorts
brushing her narrow hips.
They are young and almost wise,
they have been married four years,
have waited and saved to lean against
these starboard rails. I want to meet them as they stroll,
prudent and sly toward the stairs and small rooms.
I want to ask them questions: "Have you planned
this like everything else? What will you leave
behind because of me? What will change?"
Mom will remember the lack
of a porthole in their cabin as private,
the self-timed, palm-backdropped snapshots romantic.
Dad will remember that taxi tips were small like the islands.
But I want to know how the shape of that ice swan
returns twenty-one years later in Czech Crystal—
their gift to me for college graduation.
Even more, I want to ask,
"How much did you design,
how much was simply grace?"

Anna Elkins

Your Turn

Following the examples above, write a poem in which you re-create events leading up to your birth. You may or may not have access to any of the facts. That does not matter. Use what you know of the two parties involved to render a detailed portrait of your beginnings.

Obviously, you will need to observe standards of good taste as you write this poem. Ask yourself, How personal is too personal? How many real or imagined details do I want to disclose? The answers to these questions will probably not be clear-cut. Different people feel comfortable revealing different levels of personal information, so use your own best judgment.

Chapter Forty-Three

Revisiting the Classics

No textbook that values responses to model poems would be complete without revisiting the world of Greek and Roman mythology, for centuries a source of great themes upon which Western poets would play their variations. Therefore, your assignment for this chapter is to write a poem that reinterprets the stories of classical mythology.

In a sense, you will be writing a response to a response, for Louise Glück's poem "The Triumph of Achilles" is based on the story of Achilles, the hero of Homer's *Iliad,* and his comrade Patroclus. Briefly, the legend is as follows: The two friends fought together in the Trojan War, which lasted ten years and was waged by the Greeks in order to recapture the beautiful Helen, wife of the Greek king Menelaus. In one of the skirmishes during the Greeks' siege of Troy, Hector kills Patroclus. Although he is famed as a warrior, Achilles is so overcome by the death of his companion that he leaves the battlefield to sulk in his tent. He does eventually return to the fight, but Achilles is, as Glück suggests, "already dead," for Paris, the Trojan who started the war by abducting Helen, will soon shoot an arrow at Achilles's one vulnerable spot, his heel.

The relationship of Patroclus and Achilles has long been used, as it is here by Glück, to comment on the intensity of true friendship. While she might have chosen to dwell on the pleasures of camaraderie, Glück instead concentrates on the devastating sadness that results when one friend loses another. "What," she asks rhetorically, speaking from Achilles's point of view, "were the Greek ships on fire / compared to this loss?"

The Triumph of Achilles	In the story of Patroclus no one survives, not even Achilles who was nearly a god. Patroclus resembled him; they wore the same armor.

Always in these friendships
one serves the other, one is less than the other:
the hierarchy
is always apparent, though the legends
cannot be trusted—
their source is the survivor,
the one who has been abandoned.

What were the Greek ships on fire
compared to this loss?

In his tent, Achilles
grieved with his whole being
and the gods saw

he was a man already dead, a victim
of the part that loved,
the part that was mortal.

Louise Glück

Much of the world's great early written poetry is concerned with what we now think of as myths, but which at the time seemed very real to the people writing about them. The Mesopotamian *Epic of Gilgamesh,* Homer's *Iliad* and *Odyssey,* Virgil's *Aeneid,* the Indian *Mahabharata* and *Ramayana* are all stories in verse about archetypal heroes that also help establish social values for the citizens of those cultures. The relationship between poetry and myth is, therefore, a long and illustrious one. In fact, for most of the history of English poetry, references to **classical mythology** were considered appropriate, if not downright necessary, in a lyric poem. Talking about the gods and goddesses of Greek and Roman religion demonstrated that the poet had a proper education and respected the great literature that had come before him.

Andrea Liedtke makes a place for herself in that long tradition. Her "Artemis Explained" does just that: it describes and comments on the goddess's family relationships—she is the daughter of Zeus and twin sister of Apollo—as well as her many duties: she is the huntress for the gods, the slayer of Niobe's children (see Andrea's reference to the "good mortal harvest" in the second stanza), and the "overseer of childbirth." Unlike her fun-loving father and brother, Artemis is serious and hard-working. Andrea uses the contrast between the two genders to imply that the goddess's many laborious tasks may make her a fitter ruler than the male gods who delegated the work to her: "A disquieting thought the gods preferred to dismiss."

Artemis Explained

The goddesses on Mt. Olympus
     were charged
By father and husband and brother gods
     with miscellaneous duties
as assigned;
Forced to become omnifariously resourceful
Lest they come to bad, if spectacular, ends
At the hands of their male brethren.

Artemis was typical;
Dutiful daughter to Zeus,
god of all gods,
And dark twin to the light and artistic Apollo.
While her father made merry
     with innumerable women,
And her brother made idle gods mirthful
     with music,
She hied to the hunt,
     the gods' chief provider,
While, at the same time,
     she—deemed nature's protectress—
Maintained bird, beast, and stream
and mountain and meadow,
Then, without break,
     made good mortal harvest.
Finally, in a stroke of
     great godly humor
Or inimical irony,

alternatively,
Artemis was decreed overseer of childbirth,
In spite of her youth
      and her virginal status.

The gods were likely amazed
      when the underling goddess
Accomplished the myriad tasks
      she'd been given.
Perhaps in hindsight the gods even worried,
midst their gambols and gavottes,
Whether transforming goddesses
into fonts of resourcefulness
Comprised the mere act of dominion
      they'd simply presumed,
Or might serve to convince gullible goddesses
that their own powers were potent—
A disquieting thought the gods preferred to dismiss.

Andrea Liedtke

Your Turn

Write a poem about one or more figures from classical mythology. You may need to turn to a reference source to help you out. *Bullfinch's Mythology* is probably the most famous collection of Greco-Roman myths, but any library or bookstore will have others as well.

The prompt for Chapter Thirty-Three encouraged you to embrace anachronisms, but as you draft the poem for this assignment, you should avoid objects, facts, forms of speech, and so on, that are not in their proper historical time. While you obviously do not want to insult your readers, consider carefully how much your audience is likely to know about the story you tell. Which gods or goddesses should be familiar (Zeus, for instance)? For which do you need to provide extra background material? When in doubt, it is probably best to assume that your readers can use a brief refresher in classical mythology.

Chapter Forty-Four

Weather

If you write your poetry while sitting at a desk positioned near a window, you know how important weather is. In spring, the trees budding and flowers blossoming in the yard are likely to find their way into your lines. Similarly, in winter your poetry will probably show evidence of bare branches and snow. Weather affects where we live and what we do, and, quite naturally, writers respond to their environment in their work. Because descriptions of weather are one of the most enduring aspects of poetry, your assignment this time is to write a poem that foregrounds weather in some important respect.

The first thing a reader notices about David Citino's poem is that a weather forecast has been made to serve as the title. A clever hook to draw the reader into the poem, "One Hundred Percent Chance of Snow, Accumulating Six to Eight Inches by Morning" also functions as an effective summary of the poem. The speaker, surveying the scene in suburban Columbus, Ohio, during a

193

winter storm, finds everything—from parking lots to churchyards to the local rivers—buried under snow.

The frozen landscape, in which "each step [becomes] a fossil moment," inspires in him reveries of the past, which is also frozen in time. Among the "teeth and bone . . . arrayed in strata" are the speaker's grandparents whom, he believes, he will be joining soon. The finality of the forecast—there is no chance that it *will not* snow—suggests the corresponding finality of the death that awaits all of us.

One Hundred Percent Chance of Snow, Accumulating Six to Eight Inches by Morning

Snow billows over cracked blacktop
in parking lots of Kmart and Whirlpool plant,
plexiglass domed roof of Southland Mall
where young and old cluster and dissolve
in weekend conspiracies.

Snow blows over churches downtown,
each spire and arch shaped by antique disputes
concerning the shape or taste of God
obliterated now by tons of lovely nothing.

Here's my heaven: Ohio, bitter enough
to set teeth on edge and turn my face red
as litmus paper. Still, for all
our dirty profits, there's more love
than I can use, and more cold.

Near me beneath the ice run
the Olentangy and Scioto. So much
of our lives gets named by what's fallen.
I think of the ruddy women and men

whose teeth and bone lie arrayed in strata
beneath me, earth of their every fire dark
as obsidian. I step over burrows
where they weather forever's winter.
I'm coming soon, Grandparents.

My feet leave lines of script to mark
my progress, each step a fossil moment,
no two the same, lines that sing
my stride to anyone willing to follow
before this pure and ruthless beauty
disproves that I was ever here.

David Citino

Medieval Latin poems often began with the phrase **ubi sunt,** which means "where are [they]?" Poets would go on to name people or things that had passed from the earth and lament the ephemeral nature of life. "One Hundred Percent Chance of Snow" echoes this ancient theme. In the final stanzas, as he wanders through the church graveyard where his grandparents lie buried and all but forgotten, he cannot help but conclude that the "pure and ruthless beauty" of snow—and, by implication, of death—will inevitably obliterate any trace of his own journey on earth as well.

Michael Kitchen's "winter, AR" is another example of a poem with an ubi sunt motif. Like Citino, Michael uses climate to comment on mortality, contrasting the weather in his native Los Angeles with the weather in his grandmother's home state. Flying from "the el niño drizzle of sodden / & drenched / Los Angeles" to "the yellow ice sun" of a "bleak Arkansas afternoon," the speaker notices how different his grandmother's house seems in winter than it was in summer, the season of all his previous visits. The trees are now "arthritic" and "naked," the yellow jackets and fireflies lie dead in the windowsills. By the poem's conclusion, the subsequent death of other family members has left the speaker feeling as though he will "never be warm again."

No textbook on fiction writing would be complete without a section on **setting**—where and when a work of literature takes place. Because lyric poetry is often brief and elliptical, the topic is rarely covered in poetry textbooks, yet the setting of a poem can make a crucial difference in mood and tone, ultimately affecting how the reader interprets the piece.

Take, for example, the two poems in this chapter. If David Citino's poem was set far from where the speaker's grandparents were buried, much of the feeling of family continuity the poem evokes would disappear. And, obviously, *when* the poem occurs is imperative. A 100-degree day in July would hardly arouse the same set of emotions as snowy winter.

Likewise, setting is critical to Michael Kitchen's poem. The fact that the speaker is returning from a megalopolis, where his father had immigrated, to a country town, where his roots are, encourages us to feel that he is going home. Had he been moving from a rural to an urban setting, the sense of nostalgia would be less intense. And, as in Citino's model poem, the bleak season during which this reminiscence takes places sets the overall tone of Michael's variation.

winter, AR

when my grandmother died/
the 26th of January/
it would have been a great disrespect
not to attend the funeral
though it was a thousand miles away/

so
I pulled on my thermals/
wool slacks/
peacoat over blazer & tie/

slipped my gloves & knit cap
into the inside pocket
& wrapped a grey flannel scarf around my neck/
drove through the el niño drizzle of sodden
& drenched
Los Angeles
to the airport
& caught a flight to Little Rock/

fear of death
more than flying
cooled my palms
as I held onto the calm ride/
I walked out
into the ice
nothing on the ground
but the air cutting into the lungs anyway/
arthritic brown branches of naked trees
gnarled into the sky where I had just been
& pointed the way back/

my auntie
took me to the old house
where I'd summered
as a kid/
this was the first time I had been there
in winter
& the yellow jackets & fireflies I remembered had died
    during the fall/
caught in window screens or arrested in flight with an
    aerosol spray/

I ate some unheated leftovers
from the neighbors' kindness
with my relatives
& tried to sleep or at least lie quietly
with several blankets piled over me
before bearing the weight of the clothes again the next
    morning
standing with my cousins next to the porch swing/
our breaths smoked without cigarettes/

at the church
the Reverend Blood's words were frozen & memorized/

I noticed in the announcement that I was a pallbearer/
no one had told me/
I held the handle at the back of the casket
with blue fingers
& trundled to the hearse/
then at the cemetery I helped them lift her to the hole/
my brown ears reddened in the slight wind
& my cousin Patrice shivered
so I put my black coat
over her shoulders
& she tugged it in/

the yellow ice sun
didn't comfort me
while the others sat at table & I walked in the bleak
    Arkansas afternoon/
the severe weather made my head ache
as if I'd been swimming in an arctic surf/

inside of two years
my uncle had died
& my mother
& my uncle's wife
& now my mother's mother

& I didn't know the people I was with anymore
& I was stiff
with nothingness
& felt I would never be warm again/

Michael C. Kitchen

Your Turn

Write a poem in which the weather is an essential element. It need not be the central focus, but it should be necessary to the piece as a whole. If the temperature is especially cold or hot, think of a metaphor or simile that will convey those extremes in a fresh, surprising way. Other climatic features that you may want to work into your poem include humidity, wind speed, cloudiness, precipitation (which includes hail and sleet), thunder and lightning, and fog. The weather is likely to carry some symbolic freight in regard to the rest of the poem, but try not to be too heavy-handed with your symbolism.

Ghosts

In Chapter Forty-Five, you are asked to write a poem about ghosts. Initially, you may think of this as an invitation to create a scenario that features white sheets and rattling chains, mysterious noises in the attic, and blood-curdling screams in the night. However, as the model poem and its variation show, your poem about ghosts need not (and should not) read like a verse treatment of an episode of *Scooby Doo.*

The model poem, Yusef Komunyakaa's "Landscape for the Disappeared," takes a situation we normally associate with authoritarian regimes in the developing world and transfers it to the American South. "The disappeared"—people in countries like El Salvador who have been killed and had their bodies destroyed or concealed by death squads—apparently also exist in Louisiana. Preserved in the peat bogs like the Grauballe Man of Ireland, these ghosts return "almost healed" but with "unanswerable / questions on their lips."

Although Komunyakaa never directly says that the people in his poem died by violence, the title, our knowledge of American history, and the appalling landscape, where corpses are "lost among Venus's-flytraps / yellowing in frog spittle & downward mire," imply that the message these ghosts bring will, indeed, spare us nothing.

Landscape for the Disappeared

Lo & behold. Yes, peat bogs
in Louisiana. The dead
stumble home like swamp fog,
our lost uncles & granddaddies
come back to us almost healed.
Knob-fingered & splayfooted,
all the Has-been men
& women rise through nighttime
into our slow useless days.

Live oak & cypress
counting these shapes in a dance
human forms aren't made for. Faces
waterlogged into their own
pure expression, unanswerable
questions on their lips.

Dumbstruck premonitions rise
from the heckle-grass
to search us out.
Guilty, sings the screech owl.
I hear the hair keeps growing
in the grave. Here
moss lets down a damp light.

We call back the ones
we've never known, with stories
more ours than theirs.
The wind's low cry
their language, a lunar rainbow
lost among Venus's-flytraps
yellowing in frog spittle & downward mire,
guns & slot machines dumped
through the years.

Here's this lovely face so black
with marsh salt. Her smile,
a place where minnows swim.
All the full presence
shiny as a skull under the skin.
Say it again—we are
spared nothing.

Yusef Komunyakaa

♠

Throughout this book, you are advised to avoid clichés. Yet Pulitzer Prizewinning author Yusef Komunyakaa begins his poem with the phrase "Lo & behold," a biblical expression that long ago passed into the realm of banality. How can he justify this?

We do not know for sure what he would say, of course, but Komunyakaa *might* argue that he starts with a cliché in order to subvert it later on. The problem with clichés, of course, is that they originally did their work very well—too well, in fact. We have heard them so often that all their clarity has been worn away, like a coin that has lost its features from having been handled too many times. "Lo & behold," which asks us to observe what follows extra carefully ("lo" is an archaic form of "look"), is a remark we would normally ignore. However, immediately after using it, the poet provides us with such unusual and unforgettable imagery that the cliché is transformed and the grandeur of the biblical context is nearly revived.

We do not know whether another expression might have been just as effective, but Komunyakaa shows us that, on rare occasions, it *is* possible to use clichés effectively, as long as they are employed very sparingly and for conscious effect. A cliché that the author does not notice and deal with can "haunt" a poem just as thoroughly as the ghosts in "Landscape for the Disappeared" haunt Komunyakaa's Louisiana.

Sarah Brown's poem looks at a gentler sort of ghost. Speaking in voices that "don't often make much sense," the ghosts call out to her "in the moments before / [she is] fully awake." She speculates at first that the voices may be coming from the Ouija board in her closet. In the third stanza, she considers the possibility that she is hearing the ghosts of former pets. Finally, though, she realizes that these are the voices from the books of her childhood and, ironically, Sarah's ghosts are not interested in her at all.

The Voices

They don't often make much sense.
Sometimes just a vaguely familiar
phrase like "wrinkle" or "terabithia"
or "rainbow valley" is clear,
but their conversation seems
lively in the moments before
I am fully awake.

When they are loud,
they are sometimes on the
startling side and send me
running to the empty silence
of glow-in-the-dark
angels in my sister's
Christian room
across the hall.

I used to think it was the
Ouija board spelling out
my doom in a demonic council
from its aged cheese cloth
wrapping in the back of my closet.

Or maybe it was the chattering of
the many hamsters who have died
quite violently on my carpet—
blaming me for their eviscerations
in the jaws of my overly friendly
Yorkshire Terrier.

Years of listening, though, snatched
from the dusk between sleeping
and waking have shown me that
The Voices are absorbed in their
own lives, not mine, although my
interests have given them leave to
share my space.

Their occasional familiarity stems
from my having read their scripts, their
dialogues masterfully crafted in the
tomes upon my shelves.

Sarah Brown

Your Turn

Write a poem about ghosts. Your poem, like Komunyakaa's and Sarah's, should be set in a familiar landscape. This will help you avoid resorting to the hackneyed imagery of Halloween. You may want to consider the following questions as you write: Did you know these ghosts? Are they angry or forgiving? What do they look like? Are you frightened or pleased by their appearance? What have they come back to tell you? What do they want you (or us) to do?

Theft

The history of European interaction with the native peoples of North and South America is long, sad, and familiar. The tale is one of brutality, lies, and devastation by disease. It is also a story of theft and, according to Wendy Rose, that theft continues to the present day. While your poem for this chapter may not concern itself with larger issues like white–Native American relations, you should write a poem that describes the theft of something significant.

"For the White Poets Who Would Be Indian" is an angry poem and, given the nature of much of her other work, it is probably not a mistake to identify the speaker of the poem closely with Wendy Rose herself. Rose, who is descended from the Hopi and Miwok tribes, has written, "Without a Hopi mother, I am not even part of a clan. Learning all of this had a great deal to do with my writing poetry. How can you hope to speak if you have no voice?"

Yet even if kinship customs dictate that she not be part of a Hopi clan, Rose clearly feels herself more in touch with Native American culture than those white poets who merely seek "a temporary tourism / of [Indian] souls." She roundly condemns these interlopers, who paint their faces and chew doeskin in the hope of gaining "instant and primal" knowledge. For Wendy Rose, a person's roots are necessarily enduring and deep, not something to be ignored once "You finish your poem / and go back." Her poem is a manifesto of Native American pride and self-determination.

For the White Poets Who Would Be Indian

just once
just long enough
to snap up the words
fish-hooked
from our tongues.
You think of us now
when you kneel
on the earth,
turn holy
in a temporary tourism
of our souls.
With words
you paint your faces,
chew your doeskin,
touch breast to tree
as if sharing a mother
were all it takes,
could bring
instant and primal
of knowledge.
You think of us only
when your voice
wants for roots,
when you have sat back
on your heels
and become primitive.
You finish your poem
and go back.

Wendy Rose

In Rose's poem, the white poets invade sacred Indian land; in order to improve their own bland verse, they "fish-hook" language from Native American poets. "For the White Poets Who Would Be Indian" deals with issues of physical and emotional property, as does Jenny King's variation, entitled "What You Took." If Jenny's poem does not condemn an entire subgroup of people the way Rose's does, Jenny is nevertheless nearly as angry as her model. For Jenny, the would-be thief of this property is her ex-husband. He is forced to return the material things he stole but, to the speaker's chagrin, he retains the one intangible she desperately wants back.

Jenny's sarcastic dismissal of her ex-husband's two friends in "What You Took" as "those two / beer bellies" offers us an opportunity to talk about a special type of figurative language. **Synecdoche** is a figure of speech in which a part of something is used to describe the whole thing, or vice versa. Obviously, the beer bellies refer to people rather than to disembodied stomachs. A related type of metaphor, **metonymy,** occurs when the name of an attribute or thing is used to signify another thing with which it has become associated. When we say, "A life on the stage," for instance, we know that "the stage" really means acting or some other theatrical profession. Similarly, "the White House" refers to the president and his staff, while "the crown" refers to a king, queen, or the monarchy in general.

What You Took

California is a "community
property state," so everything
belonged equally

to both of us.
When you and those two
beer bellies backed in

that U-Haul one spring morning
while I was at my sister's
in Santa Barbara and loaded it up

as all our neighbors gaped,
you became a thief.
You stole half

our good china,
the dining room table,
the La-Z-Boy

with the back massager,
all the CDs I loved best,
you even took

the waterbed. I thought
I'd get my revenge
when the judge made you

give everything back.
Unfortunately,
there was no court order

for the complete
and immediate return
of my heart.

Jenny King

Your Turn

In Wendy Rose's poem, white people are trying to steal the identity of Native Americans. Jenny describes the loss of property and emotional investment that she suffered in the course of a bitter divorce. Write your own poem in which someone steals something important from someone else.

When you think about it, a poem centering on theft should be easy to write, for thievery has a long, if dishonorable, history. "Thou shalt not steal" is the eighth of the Ten Commandments. And theft does not just mean burglary and robbery, but also pickpocketing and embezzlement of funds. Kleptomaniacs, people who have an impulsive need to steal, make fascinating subjects for poems. Moreover, as we have seen from the two poems in this chapter, the most grievous thefts may involve intangibles rather than material goods.

Chapter Forty-Seven

Playful Piracy

If you have ever felt that a poet you were reading wrote great individual lines but did not put them in the best possible order, this chapter's assignment should interest you. Your poem will develop a variation on a model devised by Charles Bernstein, whose "From Lines of Swinburne" takes lines from various poems by the nineteenth-century British poet Algernon Charles Swinburne and rearranges them in such a way that they form an entirely new poem. Actually, this approach may not be as radical as it first seems. Some of Swinburne's critics might argue that his lines stand so well on their own because they do not make much sense when put together.

In any case, while one may question Bernstein's claim to be the "author" of "From Lines of Swinburne," there is no denying that were it not for his reassembly of the poet's work, this particular piece would not exist. And this type of writing does raise some interesting questions about collaboration. If the poet's work is not in the public domain (i.e., if it has been published in the last 75 years), can the later poet publish the poem as his or her own work? Is this sort of collage-making as valid an art form as original composition? And what if the new author somehow improves the original author's work? Who is the real genius then?

From Lines of Swinburne

As a voice in a vision that's vanished
Perjured dark are barer accusation
Song of a pole congealed
Whose soul a mark lost in the whirling snow
The soft ken, pliant
Pierced and wrung, for us
These murmurs a nearer voice, known and smeared
Mute as mouthed.

You, then, would I come to, cling to
Cleave—if raptly my throat may be
Spun and gilts be good—Unknown
Whose vesture, soft in splendor
Pale as light, the doubt that speaks
For shadow not as am
Of fervour, broom, and slope
Sifts as shifted claims, fair then fall.

Charles Bernstein

If an intelligent mind focuses on something, no matter how disjointed it is, eventually the mind will begin to bring order to the chaos. Upon careful reading, "From Lines of Swinburne" appears to be "about" one person's attempt to communicate, to be heard. There is a voice in line 1 and a "nearer voice" reappears in the penultimate line of the first stanza. In the second stanza, the poet mentions his throat, and later, "the doubt that speaks." However, an ill-defined but ominous darkness opposes the poet's desire to articulate his thoughts. The voice is in "a vision that's vanished / Perjured dark." Although the voice murmurs, it is, in the final line of the first stanza, "Mute as mouthed." In the second stanza there is a shadow hovering above the proceedings, and even light is described as "pale." Whatever conflict is taking place, it is one that the poet seems doomed to lose. Knowing what we know about "From Lines of Swinburne," this interpretation may seem far-fetched, but any poet who has seen his work misinterpreted by critics would probably agree that *any* interpretation is necessarily subjective. (An assessment, by the way, with which Charles Bernstein would agree.)

Enthusiastic about the prompt, student Frank Avery came up with a particularly clever response to Bernstein's model. "We were reading Shakespeare's sonnets in one of my literature classes," Frank writes. "My professor mentioned that there are not as many rhymes in English as there are in other languages like Italian, so I thought I might be able to use Shakespeare for this exercise. I noticed there were some sonnets towards the end where he was playing around with puns on his name, and I decided to use one of those lines to finish it up."

Despite the fact that they all come from different sonnets, the lines in Frank's poem rhyme *ababcdcdefefgg:* he has written a Shakespearean sonnet. Granted, it would be difficult to paraphrase the poem, but Frank claims that he is taking advantage of the fact that the Bard's lines are "difficult to figure out anyway." Incidentally, the title alludes to the fact that most scholars believe Shakespeare wrote 154 sonnets. (For a fuller description of the sonnet form, see Chapter 20.)

Sonnet 155

Upon those boughs which shake against the cold,
More flowers I noted, yet I none could see;
So is my love still telling what is told
To keep an adjunct to remember thee.
Th' expense of spirit is a waste of shame,
Love is my sin, and thy dear virtue hate;
Or, if it were, it bore not beauty's name,
Thy end is truth's and beauty's doom and date.
Though I, once gone, to all the world must die,
Yet eyes this cunning want to grace their art,
To swear against the truth so foul a lie,
From whence at pleasure thou mayst come and part.
   May Time disgrace and wretched minutes kill,
   Think all but one, and me in that one *Will.*

Frank Avery

Your Turn

First, read through a book of poems by a poet whose work will lend itself to this sort of exercise. As you go along, mark lines you find interesting and original, and—this is important—which you think can stand on their own. When you have plenty of lines to choose from, rearrange them so that they make a new poem, one which you have "co-authored" with the original poet.

Avoid the temptation merely to shuffle the lines randomly. For all its obscurity, Bernstein's poem, as we have seen, does make a kind of sense. And Frank Avery's piece, which follows all of the rules of a Shakespearean sonnet, goes to even greater lengths to disguise its cut-and-paste origins. Your poem should be enigmatic rather than slipshod, suggestive rather than confused.

Chapter Forty-Eight

Photographic Memories

As you read through *Poetry Writing: Theme and Variations,* you cannot help but realize that the dominant sense for most poets is sight (with sound running a close second). However, poets cannot always travel to places that will stimulate their visual faculties, so they often look at paintings, drawings, or photographs for inspiration. In this chapter you are asked to do something of that sort by revisiting an image from your own life. This time your poem should be based on a photograph or series of photographs that represent an important moment in your past.

Garrett Hongo finds this significance in a snapshot taken when he was an infant. The epigraph to his "The Hongo Store / 29 Miles Volcano / Hilo, Hawaii" notes that the inspiration for the poem comes "*From a Photograph,*" and, in fact, the entire poem seems to be reconstructed from a single picture of the poet's skinny father, "shirtless and grinning," holding his son above his head. What is especially remarkable is the way

Hongo manages to create several scenes that take place outside the boundaries of the photo and to suggest a complex web of nuclear family relationships.

He conjures up this miniature world through the extensive use of visual cues. Just a glance at the first two stanzas shows how many striking images there are: the volcano's rumble "Thudding like the bell of the Buddhist Church"; the baby in the swaying bathinette "squalling in soapy water"; the mother carrying the baby "through the orchids, ferns, and plumeria / Of that greenhouse world behind the store." Ironically, and yet all the more impressively, Hongo manages to employ so much strong imagery even though the photograph itself is only "the size of a matchbook."

The Hongo Store/ 29 Miles Volcano/ Hilo, Hawaii
—From a photograph

My parents felt those rumblings
Coming deep from the earth's belly,
Thudding like the bell of the Buddhist Church.
Tremors in the ground swayed the bathinette
Where I lay squalling in soapy water.

My mother carried me around the house,
Back through the orchids, ferns, and plumeria
Of that greenhouse world behind the store,
And jumped between gas pumps into the car.

My father gave it the gun
And said, "Be quiet," as he searched
The frequencies, flipping for the right station
(The radio squealing more loudly than I could cry).

And then even the echoes stopped—
The only sound the Edsel's grinding
And the bark and crackle of radio news
Saying stay home or go to church.

"Dees time she no blow!"
My father said, driving back
Over the red ash covering the road.
"I worried she went go for broke already!"

So in this print the size of a matchbook,
The dark skinny man, shirtless and grinning,
A toothpick in the corner of his smile,
Lifts a naked baby above his head—
Behind him the plate glass of the store only cracked.

Garrett Hongo

The danger in "The Hongo Store" turns out to be a false alarm—a volcano that could have destroyed a town does nothing more than leave red ash in the road and crack the plate glass window of a store. The expectations we have at the beginning of the poem are unfulfilled. Similarly, the title of Jackie Mitchell's poem, "Vacation Photos," leads us to anticipate a recounting of happy times in the summer sun. Instead, after thumbing through a stack of vacation photos, the narrator of Jackie's poem has come to realize that she is always "looking away" from the photographer. The speaker insists that the real action in vacation photographs is outside the frame of what the viewer can see, away from the "iron shackle chain" of the camera. To prove her point, Jackie gives us a number of examples of what lies beyond the realm of the snapshot: there is "dirt like pumpernickel dough" to knead, and "the maintenance shed / where the sweating, muddy men / tell the stories of their children," and "the ravine / [with] gigantic leafs on the tangled trees." In short, the poet argues, the real world is far more interesting than the fabricated microcosm in a picture.

Jackie Mitchell frequently performs her work live, and she knows the value of internal rhyming as a device to remind her listeners that what they are hearing is poetry rather than prose. **Internal rhyme** is rhyme in which at least one of the words is in a place *other than at the end of the line.* Examples in "Vacation Photos" include "dimple" and "simple" in lines 2 and 3, "cheek" and "seeking" in lines 3 and 4, "eight" and "hate" in lines 6 and 7, and so on.

Poets may use internal rhyme to emphasize the poetic quality of a free-verse poem. Or they may feel it is preferable to the sing-song quality of some end-rhymed poetry. In any case, internal rhymes, like all rhymes, serve to join the two words that sound alike. Subtly or insistently, rhymes also ask the reader to think of other ways the two words might be connected.

Vacation
Photos

Looking away
over there, at the honey dimple
in the simple contour of the local's cheek.
I am seeking the bottlecaps in all this garbage.
My family smiles at the camera and I am looking away.
I am seven or eight,
and I hate the T-shirt stands,
the stench of hotdogs, and the illegible ticket stubs
that blend with the woodchip paths.
I don't want to be taking a picture.
I don't want to read the glass-plated factsheets.
What I need is to knead this dirt like pumpernickel dough,
so I won't forget it even though I will be home soon.
Don't let the picture ruin what I want to be looking at,
looking away.

This isn't a place for picture taking.
There is never a place for picture taking.

Cameras are as heavy as the iron shackle chain
when the rain's rhythm calls for dancers.
The answers you will be looking for when you long to revisit
will not rot and sit in photo albums but be in the
nerve of the palms of your hands that have squeezed the
    earth
till chunks drop from between your fingers like meteors.
The stories will be told not with a picture book and
    commentary caption,
if you recognize that the most interesting place in
the National Park is the maintenance shed
where the sweating, muddy men
tell the stories of their children in the sweating Latino
    tongue.

So I am still always looking away,
hoping to stay just one more day to
absorb this humidity, exhausted with
my own humility by their larger-than lives.
Why can't I be running away
into the ravine,
the gigantic leafs on the tangled trees,
the grocery stores,
the cafeterias
single-room bars,
break rooms and smoking lounges,
to any of these places I am looking at
as I am looking
away?

Jackie Mitchell

Your Turn

Sift through your own collection of photographs and write a poem based on one or more pictures that you find particularly evocative. What do they tell you about who you were then? Who you are now?

Be sure to take advantage of the wealth of imagery right before your eyes. As much as possible, the poem should help your reader see what you see. If, for instance, the photograph is of a family picnic, what is on the table that we would not expect to see? What season is it? What sort of clothes are people wearing? Do they appear to be enjoying themselves or is there a sense of grimness about the occasion? What has occurred before the moment was captured on film? What will take place afterwards?

Chapter Forty-Nine

First Kiss

This chapter is about first kisses. In the model poem, the speaker listens as a friend describes a first kiss. The student response focuses on the speaker's own memory of the first time she kissed a boy. Your poem, too, should concentrate on a moment that our culture has endowed with significance but that, more often than not, turns out to be something of a disappointment.

Although they focus on the same subject, the two poems in this chapter are very different in tone. Rita Dove's "Adolescence—I" glamorizes the first kiss. In the words of the speaker's friend, it is "soft as baby's skin." Perhaps because the speaker is distant from the act itself, she is able to make a potentially nerve-wracking event sound magical. Indeed, nature itself seems to be intent on making young love as appealing as possible: the grasses tickle and whisper, the air "closes over" Linda's knowing remark, a firefly appears, the sky is feathery. The world, the poem implies, becomes soft and pleasant at just the mention of a first kiss.

The words in Dove's poem often sound like what they mean; they are **ono-matopoeic.** In the examples just cited, she uses alliteration ("gra*ss-es* and wh*i*spered") and assonance ("cl*o*sed *o*ver") to emphasize the onomatopoeia. Employed skillfully, this sonic imitation can seem, to use Alexander Pope's words, "an echo to the sense," thereby reinforcing and expanding the poem's literal meaning.

Adolescence
—I

In water-heavy nights behind grandmother's porch
We knelt in the tickling grasses and whispered:
Linda's face hung before us, pale as a pecan,
And it grew wise as she said:
  "A boy's lips are soft,
  As soft as baby's skin."
The air closed over her words.
A firefly whirred near my ear, and in the distance
I could hear streetlamps ping
Into miniature suns
Against a feathery sky.

Rita Dove

There are certain events in our lives—birthdays, holidays, first kisses—that most readers will immediately connect with because they have already gone through the events themselves. This familiarity is helpful inasmuch as it allows you to set the scene quickly and take your reader straight into the action. The trick is to avoid meeting so many of your reader's expectations that your poem becomes trite. Rita Dove circumvents this trap by carefully describing the poem's setting and by inserting the surprising analogy that boys' lips are "soft as baby's skin." Kelly Janssen keeps her poem fresh by undercutting our expectations about the "romance" involved in a first kiss.

Kelly focuses on the last few minutes before something decidedly distasteful occurs. The pressure is on; all her classmates are whispering, "Today's the day." Whatever pleasure the speaker may once have anticipated from a first kiss is overwhelmed by the tension she feels. She dreads the bell that will announce the end of school for the day, and has even taken to telling an invisible friend, "This sucks." Rather than Cinderella going off to the ball, the speaker sounds more like a prisoner about to face a firing squad.

Of "First," Kelly writes: "The first boy I kissed was the Methodist pastor's son, and I was so nervous. We were the first kids in sixth grade to kiss at my school. School history!" Luckily for her readers, she remembers the event vividly and is able to transport us back to that momentous afternoon.

First

Dreading the sound
of the three-ten bell,
she glances over;
he licks his lips.
Oh, God, what
has she gotten into?
Everyone whispers,
"Today's the day."
Preacher's son,
daddy's girl;
school history right
before their eyes.
Sweaty hands
crumple a secret note,
which drops to the floor
as the shrill bell rings.
The paper wad opens
to reveal the message:
"Meet me at the tire
toys after school."
"This sucks," she mutters
to an invisible friend,
as she stumbles out
to meet her fate.

Kelly Janssen

Your Turn

Write a poem in which you describe either your own first romantic kiss or the first time you heard someone describe such a kiss to you. This event is likely to be distant in time, so take a while to re-create the scene. Where does it take place? What is the speaker thinking? How does his or her body feel? What does the other party look like? Is there anyone else around when it happens? Does the speaker know, or suspect, the kiss is coming beforehand or is it a complete surprise? Does the speaker tell anyone about the event afterwards?

Chapter Fifty

(Mis) Identification

Unfortunate consequences can can result when one person misidentifies the motives, aspirations, or realities of another person. That, at any rate, is the case in the two poems in this chapter. Your poem, too, should center on an event or series of events when mistaken identification leads to an unpleasant aftermath.

Gary Soto's "Mexicans Begin Jogging" recounts such an incident. Stupidly assuming that all people of Mexican descent must be illegal aliens, the speaker's boss tells him to run from the border patrol and hands him a dollar—an appropriately inadequate parting gift from the manager of a sweatshop. Since he figures he will be paid for following orders, Soto (the poet's use of his own name in line 6 makes the reader suspect that the narrative is autobiographical) goes along with the blunder and becomes "the wag to a short tail of Mexicans." As he runs, the speaker sardonically cheers several American icons—baseball and

217

milkshakes—as well as the sociologists who are studying him. Ironically, what should be a humiliating experience politicizes and empowers the narrator.

Mexicans Begin Jogging

At the factory I worked
In the fleck of rubber, under the press
Of an oven yellow with flame,
Until the border patrol opened
Their vans and my boss waved for us to run.
"Over the fence, Soto," he shouted,
And I shouted that I was American.
"No time for lies," he said, and pressed
A dollar in my palm, hurrying me
Through the back door.

Since I was on his time, I ran
And became the wag to a short tail of Mexicans—
Ran past the amazed crowds that lined
The street and blurred like photographs, in rain.
I ran from that industrial road to the soft
Houses where people paled at the turn of an autumn sky.
What could I do but yell *vivas*
To baseball, milkshakes, and those sociologists
Who would clock me
As I jog into the next century
On the power of a great, silly grin.

Gary Soto

The title of Gary Soto's poem sounds like a newspaper headline, perhaps one announcing a story about Mexican Americans in California taking up a specific form of physical exercise. Yet the title can also be read as an imperative: "Mexicans, begin jogging! The border patrol is after you!" Soto takes full advantage of this ambiguity to remind white Americans of their preconceptions about what they expect Mexican Americans to do and be.

If "Mexicans Begin Jogging" toys with the way that we read newspaper headlines, Jen Smith's "To the B-Boys, Please Forgive Me" immediately puts the reader into a situation that many people might find unfamiliar. Reminiscing about the South Side Chicago neighborhood she grew up in, Jen Smith writes her way to an understanding of the young men rapping on her street who had an authenticity missing from the "pop stars" who do not know "what true hip-hop is really about."

Jen's perception of the B-Boys is complicated by the fact that she herself is African American, although this complication makes for an interesting poem. The first stanza clearly establishes that her initial dislike of their music is well-founded—it is vulgar and sexist and loud—but the closing lines indicate that she has become more than a little ashamed of her former intolerance.

In both these poems the importance of a good title is obvious. Unfortunately, beginning poets often shy away from titling their poems. Some feel that no title can sufficiently summarize what happens in the poem itself. Others believe that a poem should be able to stand on its own without a title to prop it up. Still others are convinced that they have no talent for titles.

Granted, a good poem can be stunted by a very general title like "Love" or "Happiness" or "Sorrow." However, to call all your poems "Untitled" is to miss a vital opportunity to tantalize, guide, or beguile your reader. Moreover, poem titles, like song titles, make a poem instantly recognizable. When was the last time you bought a CD called "Untitled" or read such a poem in a literature anthology?

Probably the best way to find a title is to ask yourself, If I had to say what my poem was about in a few words, what would those words be? If this question does not generate an answer, look at the specifics in the poem for possibilities. In the past, poems without titles (those by Emily Dickinson are a famous example) have been given the names of their first lines. As a last resort, this remains a viable option.

To the B-Boys, Please Forgive Me

I used to hate your music, with its curse words and slang
With the bass bumpin' and the artists calling women out
    their names
As cars sped down the block, blasting the sounds
Grownfolks and kids gathering around
The rhythm overwhelming as DJs sampled and scratched
The music got stolen, the style easily snatched
The wannabes gathered and battled in the park trying to
    rhyme
Seeing them with 40s and blunts wasting their time

I used to hate that music filling the night air
As they challenged each other, Step up if you dare
I couldn't connect, didn't feel what it was about, couldn't see
Then it became commercial and pop, definitely not for me
It lost its culture, its appeal, just didn't sound right
Now I long for the b-boys to come back and rhyme in the
    summer night
Come back and school these pop stars on what true hip-hop
    is really about
To a long ago b-boy, from a present fan without a doubt

Jen Smith

Your Turn

Being mistaken for someone or something you are not can be a frustrating and frightening experience. Nevertheless, as Gary Soto's poem makes clear, it can also be enlightening: you suddenly find out what it is like to be in another person's shoes. And Jen Smith shows that a person who realizes that she has misidentified other people can occasionally come to know more about those people than she would have thought possible.

Write a poem in which you remember or imagine a situation of mistaken identity. The poem may be comic or tragic, or a little bit of both. Who are the parties involved? Why has the mistake occurred? Who, if anyone, is at fault? Can the mistake be rectified, or is it an enduring one? What are the consequences? What is at stake?

A Brief Introduction to Twentieth-Century American Poetry

The following introduction attempts to place the poets included in Poetry Writing: Theme and Variations *in context, to suggest something of their achievements, their body of work as a whole, and perhaps their relation to other poets. It makes no pretense at being comprehensive. However, it should be helpful to those who are coming to the subject with little or no previous exposure, and it may remind those who have already studied American poetry of some of the things they have forgotten.*

At the turn of the century, American literature, both poetry and prose, was still affected enormously by naturalism and realism. As their names imply, these movements emphasized the importance of realistically depicting the world. The greatest realist artist was the one who could hold up a mirror to the life of the average person, showing both the good and bad. Writers classified as naturalists also valued "objective" representation of people's attitudes and behaviors, but they tended to be more pessimistic about their characters' motives, believing that humans are compelled by greed and the brutal dictates of nature to survive at any cost.

Some of these attitudes can be seen in the first major poets of the twentieth century, **E. A. Robinson** (1869–1935) and **Robert Frost** (1874–1963). Though early on he was considered the better writer of the two (he was the winner of three Pulitzer Prizes), Robinson today is remembered mostly for a handful of anthology pieces like "Richard Cory" and "Mr. Flood's Party." Nevertheless, his work provides an unflinching look at small-town American life in the form of the enduring portrait he painted of Gardiner, Maine (disguised as Tilbury Town). Frost, of course, has become one of the most famous American poets. Indeed, poems like "Mending Wall," "The Road Not Taken," "Fire and Ice," and "Stopping by Woods on a Snowy Evening" are the sum total of what many Americans think of as poetry. Yet if most of his nonliterary audience cherishes his work for its casual wisdom and clear depiction of the natural world, Frost also has a darker, tougher side that appeals to literary critics and other poets. Ultimately, Frost won four Pulitzer Prizes for his poetry, and he read one of his poems at the inauguration of John F. Kennedy.

One of the most significant events of the early part of the century was Harriet Monroe's founding of *Poetry: A Magazine of Verse* in 1912. By the end of the decade, she had published most of the important poets of the time, including Robinson, Frost, and **Carl Sandburg** (1878–1967). With his long lines and sympathy for the working man and woman, Sandburg wrote poetry that was reminiscent of the work of Walt Whitman. However, though he was quite popular in his time, Sandburg, like Robinson, has not received the continuing critical attention of his more avant-garde contemporaries.

Among the poets we associate with literary modernism are **Wallace Stevens** (1879–1955), **William Carlos Williams** (1883–1963), **Ezra Pound** (1885–1972), **T. S. Eliot** (1888–1965), and **Hart Crane** (1899–1932). Modernism is characterized by a rejection of inherited rules and conventions and by radical experiments in form and style. In part, this experimentation was a reaction to the chaos and horror inspired by the First World War (1914–1918), which resulted in 37 million casualties and the devastation of much of Europe.

The key figure in American modernism is probably Ezra Pound. Pound was as important as much for his promotion of other poets as for his own books of poetry like *Personae* (1909), *Hugh Selwyn Mauberley* (1920), and the *Cantos,* which were published from 1925 through 1970. (Sadly, Pound was arrested for treason at the end of the Second World War, declared unfit to stand trial, and imprisoned at St. Elizabeth's Hospital in Washington, D.C., after which time he returned to Italy until his death.) His protégé, Thomas Stearns Eliot, fared much better. After the groundbreaking appearance of "The Love Song of J. Alfred Prufrock" (1915) in *Poetry,* Eliot went on to publish *The Waste Land* (1922), considered by many people to be the most influential poem in twentieth-century world literature, and the *Four Quartets* (1936–1943), which charted his conversion to Anglicanism. Eliot won the Nobel Prize for literature in 1948.

William Carlos Williams, who frequently positioned himself in opposition to Eliot and Pound, championed what he claimed were distinctly American speech patterns, as opposed to the often allusive and grandiose language of his contemporaries. In poems like "To Waken an Old Lady," "Spring and All," "The Red Wheelbarrow," and "To Elsie" (which begins with the memorable line, "The pure products of America / go crazy"), Williams writes with a precision and inventiveness few American poets have matched. Another modernist who clearly saw himself outside the realm of Eliot and Pound's direct influence was Wallace Stevens. However, as his first book of poems, *Harmonium* (1923), made manifest, Stevens's ideal audience was far different from that of Dr. Williams. Cryptic, philosophical, erudite, Stevens's poetry demands a reader with a supple intelligence and an open mind. Like Stevens, Hart Crane wrote poems that are difficult to grasp at first. Obscure, sometimes very personal symbols combine with free-associative flights of fancy, and result in poetry like that in Crane's masterpiece *The Bridge* (1930), which insists on, and repays, careful and repeated study.

The poets born a generation after Pound and Eliot are a diverse group, and they did not all come into their full powers at the same time. **W. H. Auden** (1907–1973), the most significant, received early renown with the publication of his *Poems* (1930). Auden was born in England but moved to the United States in 1939 and later became an American citizen. A master of received verse forms, Auden was a firm believer that how a poem sounded was at least as important as what it said. **Theodore Roethke**

(1908–1963) was similarly acclaimed for his handling of traditional prosody, though he also wrote extensively in free verse. Born in Michigan and working for much of his career in Seattle, Roethke struggled in sometimes bitter, sometime exquisitely graceful poems to make himself heard nationally. His greatest successes came toward the end of his life. *The Waking: Poems, 1933–1953* (1953) was a Pulitzer Prize winner, and his posthumous publications received many honors.

From his first book *Heart-Shape in the Dust* (1940) to his final, posthumous *Collected Poems* (1985), **Robert Hayden** (1913–1980) published work that is passionate yet controlled, lean yet expansive. Poems like "Night, Death, Mississippi," "Middle Passage," "El-Hajj Malik El-Shabazz (Malcolm X)," and "A Letter from Phillis Wheatley" speak out strongly against racism, but Hayden, a member of the Bahai faith, believed in universal brotherhood and was less bitter than many African-American poets who were his contemporaries. **Weldon Kees** (1914–1955) was another "poet's poet": musical, intelligent, understated, ironic, quietly dedicated to his craft. Perhaps because he had no flamboyant personality to sell, Kees was not especially successful during his career, nor has he been afterward. Nevertheless, poems like "For My Daughter" are among the high-water marks of twentieth-century poetry. Like Kees, **William Stafford** (1914–1993) was a nonconformist. He was a conscientious objector during the Second World War and worked in the civilian public service corps from 1942 to 1946. A gentle, private man, he was, many people felt, not cut out for "po-biz." Nevertheless, Stafford dutifully woke early every morning to write, and this routine produced an enormous body of work, the best of which is collected in *The Way It Is: New and Selected Poems* (1998).

Drawing on the poetic achievements of earlier African-American writers like Paul Laurence Dunbar and Charles Waddell Chesnutt, and on the ideas of theorists like W. E. B. DuBois and Alaine Locke, the poets of what has come to be called the Harlem Renaissance created a literature of remarkable depth and vitality. In an essay entitled "The New Negro" (1925), Locke spoke of a "renewed self-respect and self-dependence," which would enable the black community "to enter a new dynamic phase, the buoyancy from within compensating for whatever pressure there may be of conditions from without." The Harlem Renaissance, he acknowledged, "isn't typical but it is significant, it is prophetic."

The most famous and enduring figure to emerge from the Harlem Renaissance is undoubtedly **Langston Hughes** (1902–1967). The author of fiction and journalism, as well as poetry, Hughes's many books of verse include *The Weary Blues* (1926), *Shakespeare in Harlem* (1942), and *Fields of Wonder* (1947). One of Hughes's most significant formal innovations was the incorporation of blues lyrics into his poetry. Whether he deliberately fragmented the form, as in "The Weary Blues," or remained absolutely faithful to it, as in "Young Gal's Blues," Hughes proved that arts developed by African Americans were every bit as valid as those of European Americans. Also renowned was **Claude McKay** (1890–1948), who was born in Jamaica and immigrated to the United States in 1913. His poetry is marked by a love of his home country and a strong desire for political freedom. In addition to his work as a poet, McKay traveled around the world in support of leftist causes, and he wrote several novels and an autobiography, *A*

Long Way from Home (1937). Like McKay, **Countee Cullen** (1903–1946) was a poet of formal discipline and elegance whose verse was often written in service of social justice. Cullen's major books of poetry include *Color* (1925), *The Ballad of the Brown Girl* (1927), and *The Black Christ* (1929).

With the notable exception of Emily Dickinson (whose greatness was not fully recognized until the middle of this century), women poets in America were, until recently, largely ignored in favor of men. The twentieth century has seen that unacceptable situation change dramatically. Important women poets whose work began to be appreciated before the Second World War include **Marianne Moore** (1887–1972), **Louise Bogan** (1897–1970), **Elizabeth Bishop** (1911–1979), **Muriel Rukeyser** (1913–1980), and **Gwendolyn Brooks** (1917–). The eclectic subject matter of Marianne Moore's poetry ranged from the Brooklyn Dodgers to strange animals to crystal clocks. Eccentric without being overbearing, Moore was something of a celebrity during her lifetime. Her *Collected Poems* (1951) won the Pulitzer Prize. Louise Bogan was decidedly less acclaimed than Moore, although she, too, influenced the poetry of both women and men: in the 1930s Bogan served as poetry editor of *The New Yorker.* Her own verse was spare and highly crafted, and she often turned to mythology for her subjects. Marianne Moore took Elizabeth Bishop under her wing early on in the younger poet's career, and Moore's belief that a good poem was the result of hard work and much revision was a lesson Bishop returned to throughout her career. Bishop loved to travel and marveled at the variety of the world, from the spectacular to the mundane. Many of her poems are set in Brazil, where she lived from 1952 to 1969. *Poems* (1955) won the Pulitzer Prize. Muriel Rukeyser won the Yale Younger Poets Prize with *Theory of Flight* (1935). Unfortunately, Rukeyser's reputation with the conservative poetry establishment suffered from her political activism, and her work has not received the attention it deserves. Her thoughts on poets and poetry are collected in *The Life of Poetry* (1949), which is considered a classic and has been recently reissued. Gwendolyn Brooks was an outspoken advocate for the rights of African Americans long before it was fashionable. Her work, which often takes the form of deconstructed ballads, confronts controversial racial topics head-on. Brooks was the first African American to win the Pulitzer Prize for poetry for *Annie Allen* (1949)and she was named the poet laureate of Illinois in 1968.

Among the poets who might loosely be categorized as "confessional" are **Robert Lowell** (1917–1977), **Anne Sexton** (1928–1974), **Sylvia Plath** (1932–1963) and **James Wright** (1927– 1980). Robert Lowell was initially hailed for his mastery of traditional verse forms *Lord Weary's Castle* (1946) won the Pulitzer Prize—but in *Life Studies* (1959) Lowell abandoned strictly formal poetry for a musical free verse that would profoundly influence the next generation of poets. Lowell's subject matter was idiosyncratic, and included his Boston Brahmin family, his imprisonment as a conscientious objector during World War II and, especially, the suffering his mental illness caused him and those around him. Like Lowell, Anne Sexton suffered from mental illness. In fact, she began writing poetry after being hospitalized for suicidal depression after the birth of her first child. Sexton was cynical, unflinchingly direct, and blessed with a memorable gift for metaphor. Her numerous books include the Pulitzer

Prize–winning *Live or Die* (1966). Both Sexton and Sylvia Plath were briefly members of a writing workshop taught by Lowell in 1957. Like Sexton, Plath wrote poems that put her private torment on public display. Indeed, while she is undoubtedly a very skillful poet, it is the intensity with which she lived her brief life, as much as her poetry, that has made her something of an American icon. Plath's posthumous *Collected Poems* won the 1982 Pulitzer Prize, nearly twenty years after she committed suicide. While he was not directly in Lowell's orbit, James Wright's career paralleled Lowell's in several ways. Although he was born in a working-class family in Martin's Ferry, Ohio (the town and its people would return again and again in his poetry), Wright, too, began as a champion of traditional verse. *The Green Wall* (1957) won the Yale Younger Poets Prize, but by 1963, with *The Branch Will Not Break,* he was writing in a flexible free verse that, like Lowell's, would be highly influential. Wright's *Collected Poems* (1971) won the Pulitzer Prize.

Some of the other poets of this generation do not lend themselves as easily to the groupings made necessary by a short introduction such as this one. **Denise Levertov** (1923–1997) was born in England but emigrated to the United States in 1948. She was noted nearly as much for her political and social activism—she was antinuclear, antiwar, pro-environmental—as for her poetry. Levertov's aesthetic was shaped by the precise, imagistic poetry of William Carlos Williams, whom she greatly admired. **James Dickey** (1923–1997) is perhaps best known for his novel *Deliverance* (1970), which was made into a hit movie. However his poetry, too, has been influential, especially among Southern white males. Dickey wrote from an unashamedly masculine viewpoint, and his triumphs can be found in *Buckdancer's Choice* (1965), his most celebrated volume, as well as in his collected poems, *The Whole Motion* (1992). Like Theodore Roethke in Washington state, **Richard Hugo** (1923–1982) in Montana sometimes seemed to write from a sense of profound isolation. Yet he kept in touch with the larger literary world through the mail and by acting as an important tastemaker in American poetry. For years he served as the judge of the Yale Series of Younger Poets and his *The Triggering Town* (1979), which covers both spiritual issues and the nuts and bolts of writing, remains a staple of creative writing classrooms. **Donald Justice** (1925–) is the editor of Weldon Kees's *Collected Poems,* and some of the older poet's technical proficiency and muted irony are evident in Justice's work as well. Justice's poems are often about people dealing with lost love, lost opportunity, and lost childhood. His *Selected Poems* (1979) was awarded the Pulitzer Prize.

Two of the most famous American poets of the second half of the century emerged from the Beat movement which, ironically, had drawn much of its energy from a rejection of the "traditional" American values of the Eisenhower years. **Allen Ginsberg** (1926–1997) claimed as his two major poetic influences William Blake and Walt Whitman. Probably Ginsberg's most famous book of poetry was *Howl* (1955), which many people still consider, along with Jack Kerouac's *On the Road,* a bible of the Beat generation. Early copies of *Howl* were confiscated as obscene, although the book was later cleared of those charges in a celebrated trial. While he was never fully embraced by literary critics, Ginsberg enjoyed enormous popular success, which was cemented by readings of his poetry at venues around the world. Ginsberg's compatriot **Gary Snyder**

(1930–) never quite had the older poet's flair for the dramatic public appearance, but Snyder has always been a committed environmentalist, and his back-to-nature esthetic has drawn a wide and devoted following. Snyder's *Turtle Island* won the 1975 Pulitzer Prize.

Kenneth Koch (1925–) and **Frank O'Hara** (1926–1966) were both associated with what was called the New York School of poetry. Rejecting the standards of 1950s and early 1960s academic verse—polite, cultured and, many would say, boring—the poetry of the New York School was nevertheless more clearly the work of intellectuals (as opposed to visionaries) than that of their Beat contemporaries. Postmodernism, which by nature is slippery to define, values fragmentation and hybridity of expression and form; it questions the foundations of our dominant value systems and is skeptical of any "ultimate" meaning. Parodic, spontaneous, and responsive to pop culture, the New York School poets were among the first who might be considered postmodern. O'Hara was probably the funniest and bawdiest of these poets. Koch, too, has a wry sense of humor, and his work includes several ambitious book-length poems.

Sympathetic to the New York School but even more radical in their postmodern approach, poets identified with the Language school of poetry include **Lyn Hejinian** (1941–) and **Charles Bernstein** (1950–). Hejinian's interest in the labyrinthine complexity of Russian literature (she has translated Russian poets and one of her books, *Oxota* (1991), is inspired by Pushkin's *Eugene Onegin*) is mirrored by the intricacy of her own poetry and prose. Bernstein's poetry leaps from difficult metaphysical propositions to dubious puns and back again with an ironic fluency. He offers a fascinating explanation and defense of his own and others' experimental poetry in a collection of essays entitled *Content's Dream* (1986), and with Bruce Andrews, he co-edited *The L=A=N=G=U=A=G=E Book* (1984). Although more than a generation their senior, **John Cage** (1912–1992) worked with the Language poets and was an important precursor. Also renowned as an avant-garde artist and composer, Cage is probably best known for his (in)famous composition *4'33"* (1952), in which a performer sits at the piano for four and a half minutes doing nothing: the ambient noise in the concert hall becomes the music.

In the past thirty years, in part because of the advances made in civil rights, poets of color have gained an audience and critical following that earlier in the century would have seemed unimaginable. Writing by African Americans has especially flourished. In addition to playing an important role in the civil rights movement, **Amiri Baraka** (1934–) originally known as LeRoi Jones—is the author of plays, fiction, essays, and poetry that focus on black experience. His poems are collected in *Transbluesency* (1995). **Audre Lorde** (1934–1992), whose *Chosen Poems: Old and New* appeared in 1982, was not afraid to tackle difficult subjects: she confronted prejudice among women's groups and sexism among those championing Black Power. **Yusef Komunyakaa** (1947–) won the Pulitzer Prize for *Neon Vernacular* (1993) his selected poems, many of which deal with his experience as an "information specialist" in Vietnam. Komunyakaa is also a devoted fan of jazz, and even when he is not writing directly about the music, its cadences find their way into his rhythmic free verse. **Rita Dove** (1952–) won the Pulitzer Prize for *Thomas and Beulah* (1986), which is a re-creation of the courtship and marriage of her grandparents. She served as the United States poet laureate from 1993 to 1995.

Wendy Rose (1948–) is descended from the Hopi and Miwok tribes. Rose is an important figure in the renaissance of Native American literature, which was "officially" recognized when N. Scott Momaday's *House Made of Dawn* (1968) won the Pulitzer Prize for fiction. Rose herself has received a number of prizes, including an American Book Award from the Before Columbus Foundation. *Bone Dance: New and Selected Poems, 1965–1993,* was published in 1994. In addition to her Native American ancestry, she has explored environmental and feminist issues in her work. Though **Mary TallMountain** (1918–1994) was considerably older than Rose, she did not begin publishing until she was in her fifties, long after the younger poet had begun. After a career as a legal secretary, TallMountain met Native American poet Paula Gunn Allen, who helped make possible the publication of her most important book, *The Light on the Tent Wall: A Bridging* (1990). An Athabascan Indian who was taken from her family as a child when her mother contracted tuberculosis, TallMountain writes movingly about the clash of native and white cultures and her early years in what was then still called the Alaskan Territory.

Garret Hongo (1951–) was born in Hawaii, and the imagery of island life recurs often in his poetry. Engaged in a quest to discover his cultural and familial origins, Hongo also wants to reach out to readers of all backgrounds. He is the editor of *The Open Boat: Poems from Asian America* (1993). **Gary Soto** (1952–) likewise draws on his heritage (working-class Mexican American) to create poems of universal significance. Talented in several genres, Soto has also written autobiography, short fiction, and children's books. His *New and Selected Poems* was published in 1995.

If many poets have withdrawn into the relative safety of the academy, even there iconoclasts remain. **Billy Collins** (1941–), who teaches at Lehman College of the City University of New York, writes clever, funny, wistful poems. His work proves definitively that one can write a humorous poem without being silly. **Gerald Locklin** (1941–), a professor at California State–Long Beach and one of the most prolific poets in American history, has an equally droll perspective on the modern world. Writing in the persona of a good-hearted, if sometimes bumbling, Everyman (sometimes called "Toad"), Locklin has, in books like *The Toad Poems* (1970), *Poop, and Other Poems* (1972), *children of a lesser demagogue* (1987), and *a constituency of dunces* (1988), created one of the most distinctive voices in contemporary poetry. **David Citino** (1947–) teaches at Ohio State University, and he writes with great fondness about Ohio and his family life there. A sometimes wistful, sometimes humorous nostalgist, Citino has created one of the great literary figures of the twentieth century in Sister Mary Appassionata, a Catholic School teacher who lectures on everything from theology to human behavior to paleontology to sex education. **Pattiann Rogers** (1940–), **Sharon Olds** (1942–), and **Louise Glück** (1943–) have all taught at a variety of universities, although their interests are radically different. Rogers has made science and the natural world her primary subject matter. Titles like "Eulogy for a Hermit Crab," "Counting What the Cactus Contains," and "The Voice of the Precambrian Sea" suggest the character of her interests. The breadth and depth of her knowledge are on ample display in *Firekeeper,* her selected poems, which was published in 1994. Olds is in many ways reminiscent of the confessional poets of twenty years earlier. Her first book, *Satan Says* (1980), depicts the relationships in her immediate family with uncompromising forthrightness. Indeed, the entire body of her work, from *Satan Says* to *The Dead and the Living* (1984), winner of the Lamont Prize, to *The Wellspring* (1996) presents us with a poet deeply interested in the myriad manifestations of human psychology. Louise Glück's subject matter has ranged from classical mythology to flowers. Her 1992 volume *The Wild Iris* was a winner of the Pulitzer Prize.

The future of poetry as we move into the next century is, of course, impossible to predict. Yet if this century is any indication, American verse will consist of more, and more diverse, voices. It will find innovative ways to accommodate and transform history. And it will continue to offer beginning poets a vast range of models for their own work.

Glossary

Acrostic A form of writing in which certain letters in each line form a message when read downward in sequence. Typically, the initial letters of each line make a word. In a **mesostic,** one of the middle letters in each line can be read downward to form a word.

Alliteration The repetition of similar sounds in nearby words. Normally, the term refers to initial consonant sounds, although technically assonance is a type of alliteration.

Allusion A reference to a person, place, thing, event, or idea outside the work itself.

Anachronism A reference to something not in its proper historical time.

Anaphora The repetition of initial words or phrases in successive clauses, sentences, or stanzas. Anaphora is used to create a powerful rhythm, which helps drive home a writer's point.

Aphorism A succinct, memorable formulation; a maxim or adage.

Ars Poetica Literally, "the art of poetry." A summation of an author's ideas about how the art of poetry should be practiced. The term comes to us from the title of a famous essay by the Roman poet Horace.

Assonance The repetition of internal vowel sounds.

Ballad A narrative poem, often with a recurring refrain. There are four lines in each **ballad stanza,** the lines alternating between iambic tetrameter (four stressed syllables per line) and iambic trimeter (three stressed syllables per line), with the final words in the lines rhyming *abcb*. Among the many famous English ballads are "Sir Patrick Spens," "Lord Randal" and "The Demon Lover."

Catalog A list, sometimes descriptive, of people, places, things, or ideas.

Confessional poetry A term used to describe the work of some of the major poets of the 1950s and 1960s, including Robert Lowell, Sylvia Plath, Anne Sexton, and James Wright. Their work is especially frank in addressing their own intimate moral, emotional, and physical life.

Dialect A type of language unique to a specific regional or social group.

Diction Refers to a writer's choice of words, phrases, sentence structure, and figurative language. In everyday conversation, we tend to use **informal diction.** Classroom and business writing, which typically require a more careful selection process, call for **formal diction. Poetic diction** alludes to an elevated style of poetry that would sound ridiculous in ordinary conversation.

Dramatic monologue A poem in which the speaker takes on the identity of some person other than himself or herself. The speaker addresses a specific listener or listeners, whose replies—if there are any—we cannot hear. Typically, in the course of a dramatic monologue the person unintentionally reveals a great many things about his or her disposition, desires, fears, and flaws.

Elegy A mournful poem, especially one lamenting a person who has died.

Enjambment From the Old French word for "straddling," sometimes described as an "in-striding." Unlike **end-stopped** lines, which conclude with some form of punctuation, enjambed lines "stride over" to the next line without pausing.

Epistolary A type of literature written in the form of letters.

Free verse Poetry with no regular meter or line length.

Homage Special respect paid to someone or something.

Hyperbole Exaggerated or extravagant speech.

Imagery The "concrete," as opposed to the "abstract," in a poem. C. Day Lewis called the image "a picture made out of words." In its broader usage, "imagery" refers to appeals to the other four senses as well: taste, touch, sound, and smell.

Imagist movement An early twentieth-century literary movement that valued precise imagery in poetry, freedom in the choice of subject matter, and an avoidance of excessive sentimentality.

Irony The incongruity created by the difference between appearance and reality. **Verbal irony** occurs when people use words to convey the opposite of what they mean. **Dramatic irony** takes place when characters in a work of literature are unaware of what the audience knows. In **situational irony** there is a discrepancy between what we expect to happen under certain circumstances and what actually happens.

Language poetry An experimental movement that emerged in the 1970s and values playful irony, fragmentation, subjectivity, and "open" forms. Language poets have expressed an interest in scattering words, phrases, and sentences on the page, believing that the unexpected juxtapositions they create reveal more about life at the end of our chaotic century than more traditional, less imaginative poems.

Line The basic unit of composition in poetry. A line stretches from the left margin to the right margin, where the **line break** occurs.

Lyric poem A brief poem that expresses a speaker's thoughts and emotions and does not attempt to tell an extended story.

Metaphor A figure of speech in which a word or phrase that ordinarily denotes one thing is applied to something else in order to suggest an analogy or likeness between the two. I. A. Richards coined the terms **tenor** for the subject to which a metaphor is applied and **vehicle** for the metaphoric term itself.

Meter The arrangement of words in a poem based on the relative stress of their syllables. The act of counting the number of stressed and unstressed syllables is called **scansion.** The basic metrical unit, consisting of two or three syllables, is the **foot.** The names of the most common feet (_ represents an unaccented syllable and / represents an accented syllable) are as follows:

> iamb (iambic): _ /
> trochee (trochaic): / _
> anapest (anapestic): _ _ /
> dactyl (dactylic): / _ _
> spondee (spondaic): / /
> pyrrhic (pyrrhic): _ _

Line lengths are also given specific names:

> monometer: one foot
> dimeter: two feet
> trimeter: three feet
> tetrameter: four feet
> pentameter: five feet
> hexameter: six feet
> heptameter: seven feet
> octameter: eight feet

In a **rising meter** the syllables in each foot go from unstressed to stressed; a **falling meter** moves from stressed to unstressed syllables. The most common of all English verse forms is unrhymed iambic pentameter, or **blank verse.**

Metonymy A figure of speech in which the name of an attribute of a thing is substituted for the thing itself, as in "the Crown" for the monarchy.

Multiculturalism The belief that an ideal society is one that values the ideas and opinions of as diverse a group of women and men as possible.

Narrative poem A poem that tells a story.

Neologism A newly coined, sometimes meaningless word or phrase.

Objective correlative A term coined by T. S. Eliot that refers to an object or situation that evokes a particular set of emotions in a reader.

Onomatopoeia The use of words whose sounds mimic their meanings.

Performance poetry Poetry that is performed aloud. Typically, poets memorize their work and employ a well-rehearsed delivery, sometimes incorporating actors' gestures, and even stage props into their presentations. An event where such performances take place is sometimes called a **poetry slam.**

Personification The act of endowing an abstraction or an inanimate object with living characteristics or with human attributes and feelings.

Political poetry Poetry that seeks to change or confirm the reader's opinion on a public matter.

Prewriting That informal part of the writing process which takes place before a writer begins to compose with a final product in mind. Two of the most frequently used strategies are freewriting and clustering (also called brainstorming). **Freewriting** involves writing nonstop, for a short, predetermined period of time. **Clustering,** or **brainstorming,** encourages writers to jot down words and phrases and then to look for patterns or connections in what they have written down.

Prose poem Poetry written in the form of prose, i.e., without recourse to line breaks. Ideally, it is rhythmic, compact, and imagistic. Often the language of the prose poem is surreal and/or experimental in nature.

Refrain A phrase, line, or group of lines, repeated at intervals.

Rhyme Similarity of the terminal sounds of words. The **rhyme scheme** is the pattern of rhyming words in a poem. In a **perfect rhyme** the final vowel and consonant sounds are the same. In a **slant,** or **near, rhyme** the sounds are nearly, but not precisely, alike. A **sight,** or **eye, rhyme** looks as though it should rhyme exactly, but does not. An **internal rhyme** is one in which at least one of the rhyming words is in a place other than at the end of the line.

Sentimentality An extravagant display of emotion, romance, pity, or sympathy.

Simile A figure of speech that states a likeness between two unlike things, usually with words such as *like, as,* or *seems.*

Setting The place, time and social circumstances in which a work of literature takes place.

Soliloquy A form of address in which a person talks to himself or herself as though thinking aloud but is unable to be heard by other characters.

Sonnet A fourteen-line poem written in iambic pentameter. In the **Italian,** or **Petrarchan, sonnet** (which was supposedly perfected by the fourteenth-century Italian poet Petrarch), there is an eight-line **octave** followed by a six-line **sestet.** Traditionally, the octave develops an idea, which the sestet completes. The turning point between the two parts is called the *volta.* The Petrarchan rhyme scheme is an *abbaabba* octave with a *cdecde* sestet (or some variation on those three rhymes). An **English,** or **Shakespearean, sonnet** consists of fourteen lines of iambic pentameter, with three quatrains—which rhyme *abab cdcd efef*—followed by a rhyming couplet.

Stanza The poetic equivalent of the paragraph in prose. Among the many types of stanzas are **couplets** (pairs of lines, both rhyming and nonrhyming), **tercets** (three-line stanzas), and **quatrains** (four-line stanzas).

Style The distinctive way that a writer has of expressing herself in poetry, including everything from tone and diction to syntax and use of metaphor.

Symbol Something that represents something else, and that may inspire a number of additional meanings beyond its literal significance.

Synecdoche A figure of speech in which a part of something is used to describe the whole thing.

Syntax The way in which words or phrases are combined to form a sentence.

Syllabics A method of composing poetry in which the poet counts the total number of syllables per line rather than the number of accented syllables.

Tone The speaker's manner of expression or attitude toward his listener or subject.

Ubi sunt A phrase often appearing in medieval poems, which translates as "where are [they]?" Poems with an *ubi sunt* theme lament the passing of time and the ephemeral nature of life.

Verisimilitude The quality of appearing real or true.

Villanelle A French form that consists of five tercets and a final quatrain. The first and third lines of the first tercet recur alternately in all subsequent tercets and become the final couplet in the quatrain. The rhyme scheme in the tercets is *aba,* and the second lines of all stanzas rhyme with each other. The quatrain rhymes *abaa.*

Voice The means, real or adopted, by which a poet conveys a sense of self and/or creates a particular tone and mood.

Acknowledgments

Auden, W. H. From *W.H. Auden: Collected Poems* by W.H. Auden, edited by E. Mendelson. Copyright © 1940 and renewed 1968 by W.H. Auden. Reprinted by permission of Random House, Inc., and Faber and Faber Ltd.

Baraka, Amiri. "Buddha Asked Monk," by Amiri Baraka from *Funk Lore: New Poems (1984–1995)*. Reprinted by permission of Sterling Lord Literistic, Inc. Copyright 1995 by Amiri Baraka.

Bernstein, Charles. From *The Sophist* (Los Angeles: Sun & Moon Press, 1987) p. 37 © 1987 by Charles Bernstein. Reprinted by permission of the publisher.

Bishop, Elizabeth. "Questions of Travel" from *The Complete Poems 1927–1979* by Elizabeth Bishop. Copyright © 1979, 1983 by Alice Helen Methfessel. Reprinted by permission of Farrar, Straus & Giroux, Inc.

Bogan, Louise. "The Dragonfly" from *Blue Estuaries* by Louise Bogan. Copyright © 1968 by Louise Bogan. Reprinted by permission of Farrar, Straus & Giroux, Inc.

Brooks, Gwendolyn. "A Bronzeville Mother Loiters in Mississippi, Meanwhile, A Mississippi Mother Burns Bacon" by Gwendolyn Brooks © 1991, as published in her book *Blacks* © 1991 published by Third World Press, Chicago.

Cage, John. "25 Mesostics Re and Not Re Mark Tobey" from *M: Writings '67–72* © 1973 by John Cage, Wesleyan University Press, by permission of University Press of New England.

Citino, David. "One Hundred Percent Chance of Snow, Accumulating to Six to Eight Inches by Morning" by David Citino from *The Discipline: New and Selected Poems 1980–1992*. Copyright 1992 by the Ohio State University Press. Reprinted by permission.

Collins, Billy. "Putting Down the Cat" by Billy Collins from *The Apple That Astonished Paris*. Reprinted by permission of the University of Arkansas Press. Copyright 1988 by Billy Collins.

Crane, Hart. "To Brooklyn Bridge," from *Complete Poems of Hart Crane* by Marc Simon, editor. Copyright © 1993, © 1958, 1966 by Liveright Publishing Corporation. Copyright © 1986 by Marc Simon. Reprinted by permission of Liveright Publishing Corporation.

Cullen, Countee. "Incident" by Countee Cullen from *Color* © 1925 Harper & Bros., NY. Renewed 1952 by Ida M. Cullen. Copyrights administered by Thompson and Thompson, New York, NY.

Dickey, James. "The Celebration" from *The Whole Motion: collected poems, 1945–1992* © 1992 by James Dickey, Wesleyan University Press by permission of University Press of New England.

Dove, Rita. "Adolescence—I," © 1980 Rita Dove. From *The Yellow House on the Corner,* Carnegie-Mellon University Press. Reprinted by permission of the author.

Eliot, T. S. "Journey of the Magi" from *Collected Poems 1909–1962* by T. S. Eliot, copyright 1936 by Harcourt Brace & Company, copyright © 1964, 1963 by T. S. Eliot, reprinted by permission of Harcourt Brace & Company, and Faber & Faber Ltd.

Ginsberg, Allen. All lines from "Café in Warsaw" from *Collected Poems 1947–1980* by Allen Ginsberg. Copyright © 1965 by Allen Ginsberg. Reprinted by permission of HarperCollins Publishers, Inc.

Glück, Louise. "The Triumph of Achilles" from *The Triumph of Achilles* by Louise Glück. Copyright © 1985 by Louise Glück. Reprinted by permission of The Ecco Press.

Hayden, Robert. "Those Winter Sundays," copyright © 1966 by Robert Hayden, from *Collected Poems of Robert Hayden* by Frederick Glaysher, editor. Reprinted by permission of Liveright Publishing Corporation.

Hejinian, Lyn. *My Life* (Los Angeles: Sun & Moon Press, 1987) pp. 50 and 51. © 1987, 1980 by Lyn Hejinian. Reprinted by permission of the publisher.

Hongo, Garrett Kaoru. "The Hongo Store" from *Yellow Light* © 1982 by Garrett Kaoru Hongo, Wesleyan University Press by permission of University Press of New England.

Hughes, Langston. "The Weary Blues" from *Collected Poems* by Langston Hughes. Copyright © 1994 by the Estate of Langston Hughes. Reprinted by permission of Alfred A. Knopf, Inc.

Hugo, Richard. "Letter to Ammons from Maratea," copyright © 1977 by Richard Hugo, from *Making Certain It Goes on: The Collected Poems of Richard Hugo* by Richard Hugo. Reprinted by permission of W.W. Norton & Company, Inc.

Justice, Donald. "Variations for Two Pianos" from *New and Selected Poems* by Donald Justice. Copyright © 1995 by Donald Justice. Reprinted by permission of Alfred A. Knopf, Inc.

Kees, Weldon. "For My Daughter," reprinted from *The Collected Poems of Weldon Kees,* edited by Donald Justice, by permission of the University of Nebraska Press. Copyright © 1975, by the University of Nebraska Press.

Koch, Kenneth. "To You" by Kenneth Koch from *On the Great Atlantic Rainway: Selected Poems 1950–1988.* Copyright © 1994 by Kenneth Koch. Reprinted by permission.

Komunyakaa, Yusef. "Landscape for the Disappeared" from *Neon Vernacular* © 1993 by Yusef Komunyakaa, Wesleyan University Press by permission of the University Press of New England.

Levertov, Denise. "Williams: An Essay" by Denise Levertov, from *Candles in Babylon.* Copyright © 1982 by Denise Levertov. Reprinted by permission of New Directions Publishing Corp.

Locklin, Gerald. "a constituency of dunces" from *a consituency of dunces* by Gerald Locklin, Slipstream Press, copyright © 1988 by Gerald Locklin. Reprinted by permission of the author.

Lorde, Audre. "The Brown Menace Or Poem To The Survival Of Roaches," copyright © 1974 by Audre Lorde, from *Collected Poems* by Audre Lorde. Reprinted by permission of W.W. Norton & Company, Inc.

Lowell, Robert. "Skunk Hour" from *Life Studies* by Robert Lowell. Copyright © 1959 by Robert Lowell. Copyright renewed © 1987 by Harriet Lowell, Sheridan Lowell, and Caroline Lowell. Reprinted by permission of Farrar, Straus & Giroux, Inc.

McKay, Claude. "If We Must Die" from *Selected Poems of Claude McKay.*

Moore, Marianne. "The Steeple-Jack," copyright 1951 © 1970 by Marianne Moore, © renewed 1979 by Lawrence E. Brinn and Louise Crane, Executors of the Estate of Marianne Moore, from *The Complete Poems of Marianne Moore* by Marianne Moore. Used by permission of Viking Penguin, a division of Penguin Putnam, Inc.

O'Hara, Frank. "Poem: Lana Turner Has Collasped" from *Lunch Poems* by Frank O'Hara. Copyright © 1964 by Frank O'Hara. Reprinted by permission of City Lights Books.

Olds, Sharon. "I Go Back to May 1937" from *The Gold Cell* by Sharon Olds. Copyright © 1987 by Sharon Olds. Reprinted by permission of Alfred A. Knopf, Inc.

Plath, Sylvia. All lines from "Blackberrying" from *Crossing the Water* by Sylvia Plath. Copyright © 1962 by Ted Hughes. Copyright Renewed. This poem originally appeared in *Uncollected Poems,* Turret Books, London, and in *Hudson Review.* Reprinted by permission of HarperCollins Publishers, Inc. and Faber & Faber, Ltd.

Pound, Ezra. "A Pact" by Ezra Pound, from *Personae.* Copyright © 1926 by Ezra Pound. Reprinted by permission of New Directions Publishing Corp.

Roethke, Theodore. "Elegy for Jane," copyright 1950 by Theodore Roethke. From *The Collected Poems of Theodore Roethke* by Theodore Roethke. Used by permission of Doubleday, a division of Bantam Doubleday Dell Publishing Group, Inc.

Rogers, Pattiann. "Suppose Your Father Was a Redbird" was published in *Firekeeper: New and Selected Poems* by Pattiann Rogers (Milkweed Editions, 1994). Copyright © 1994 by Pattiann Rogers. Reprinted with permission from Milkweed Editions, Minneapolis, MN, (800) 520-6455.

Rose, Wendy. "For the White Poets Who Would Be Indian" by Wendy Rose from *Lost Copper* by Wendy Rose and N. Scott Momaday. Reprinted courtesy of Malki Museum, Inc. Copyright © 1980 Malki Museum, Inc.

Rukeyser, Muriel. "Waiting for Icarus" by Muriel Rukeyser, from *A Muriel Rukeyser Reader,* 1994, W.W. Norton, New York City, © William Rukeyser.

Sandburg, Carl. "Chicago" from *Chicago Poems* by Carl Sandburg, copyright 1916 by Holt, Rinehart and Winston and renewed 1944 by Carl Sandburg, reprinted by permission of Harcourt Brace & Company.

Sexton, Anne. "Cinderella" from *Transformations.* Copyright © 1971 by Anne Sexton. Reprinted by permission of Houghton Miflin Co. All rights reserved.

Snyder, Gary. "I Went into the Mavrick Bar" by Gary Snyder, from *Turtle Island.* Copyright © 1974 by Gary Snyder. Reprinted by permission of New Directions Publishing Corp.

Soto, Gary. "Mexicans Begin Jogging," by Gary Soto from *New and Selected Poems* by Gary Soto. © 1981. Reprinted by permission of Chronicle Books, San Francisco.

Stafford, William. "At the Un-National Monument along the Canadian Border" copyright 1977, 1998 by the Estate of William Stafford. Reprinted from *The Way It Was: New & Selected Poems* by William Stafford with the permission of Graywolf Press, Saint Paul, Minnesota.

Steven, Wallace. "Anecdote of the Jar" from *Collected Poems* by Wallace Stevens. Copyright 1923 and renewed 1951 by Wallace Stevens. Reprinted by permission of Alfred A. Knopf, Inc.

TallMountain, Mary. "Matmiya" by Mary TallMountain is reprinted from *Light on a Tent Wall,* by permission of the American Indian Studies Center, UCLA. © Regents of the University of California.

Williams, William Carlos. "This is Just to Say" by William Carlos Williams, from *Collected Poems: 1909–1939,* Volume I. Copyright © 1938 by New Directions Publishing Corp.

Wright, James. "Autumn Begins in Martin's Ferry, Ohio," from *Above the River: The Complete Poems* © 1990 by Anne Wright, Wesleyan University Press, by permission of University Press of New England.

Index